KEN DAVIS

Lighten Up and Live

BroadStreet
PUBLISHING

BroadStreet Publishing Group LLC
Racine, WI 53403
Broadstreetpublishing.com

Lighten Up and Live!

ISBN 978-1-4245-4941-2

Design by Chris Garborg | garborgdesign.com
Illustrations by Greg Scott

Printed in China

CONTENTS

ACKNOWLEDGMENTS

Sincere thanks to my management team Joy Groblebe and Brian Scheer for encouraging me to write this devotional.

A special thanks to Drew Blankman, who edited my writing and made suggestions that made these devotionals more powerful and clear. He made the editing process fun.

I also wish to thank Mike Atkinson and Mikey's Funnies for being an amazing resource for many of the clean jokes and stories used in this book.

We worked diligently to search for the authors or originators of each of these stories. Where we were successful, the sources are footnoted. If you find we have missed the original source of a story, please let us know and we will correct it.

Blessing to you! I truly hope this book will brighten your days.

How to Use This Book

Devotionals come in a variety of forms. This devotional is designed to use humor to drive home wonderful truths from God's Word. I find my day goes better if it starts with a smile, and better yet, if I focus on some aspect of God's Word to apply during the day.

These 90 devotionals should not replace your regular Bible study. They were written with the hope they might inspire you to a deeper appreciation of God's Word and the desire to study it.

- Share a devotional each morning or evening with y our family.
- Make it fun. Share similar jokes and stories.
- Pray together about the topic of the devotional.
- Take advantage of the opportunity to "Go Deeper" when it is offered.
- Report back to each other on how God used a particular devotional in your life.

I pray that God will hear the sound of laughter as you read these, and that He will touch your heart with the point of the devotional and inspire families to get into His Word. May these stories and the scriptures that accompany them bring joy to your life. Lighten up and live!

DISTRACTIONS

A couple was having a party at their house. An hour before the party, the woman found out that she still needed escargot—an entrée made from snails. So, she sent her husband to get it.

On the way, he passed the golf course and decided to rent some clubs and hit some balls on the driving range. An hour and a half later, he looked at his watch and realized that the party had already started. He quickly ran to the market, bought a bucket of snails and drove home.

He tried to sneak into the kitchen without his wife seeing him, but he stumbled and spilled the snails all over the floor. Hearing the noise, his wife stormed into the room. Without hesitation he looked down and shouted, "Come on guys, we're almost there!"

The problem of being distracted from the main task is common to all of us. It is especially acute with people my age. It's not a big deal if you are cleaning your desk and end up reading a book, but it's crucial if you are distracted from your purpose for living. Living with no regrets means staying focused on your goal.

Set your goal high and stay on track.

Paul says, *"I press on toward the goal to win the prize for which God has called me heavenward in Christ Jesus" (Philippians 3:14).*

Don't let anything distract you from that calling. At the end of your life there will be no time to blame the snails.

Go Deeper: Philippians 3:7-14

GETTING ALONG

On the way to church my children would sit in the back seat picking fights over senseless things.

"This is my side of the car!" one would yell. "You are breathing on my side of the car."

"She's looking at me!" the other would counter.

I would grab the rearview mirror and give them "the Sunday morning look of love," an unmistakable glare warning of the catastrophic consequences if the battle continued. That would be followed by a lecture peppered with questions that had no rational answer.

"Do you want me to come back there?"

"Do you know what will happen if I stop this car?"

Swatting at them was not an option because all children are born with the innate knowledge of the one spot in the car your arm can never reach.

Most of my life I struggled to figure out how to discipline a child while driving, until an old gentleman pulled me aside and whispered, "A touch on the brakes brings them right into play."

Unfortunately, the same kind of quibbling can follow us into adult life with disastrous results: church splits, destroyed relationships, bitterness and revenge.

In Romans 12, the apostle Paul gave this instruction to believers: *"Do not repay anyone evil for evil. Be careful to do what is right in the eyes of everyone. If it is possible, as far as it depends on you, live at peace with everyone" (vv. 17-18).*

If that doesn't work, there is always the brakes.

Go Deeper: Romans 12:9-21

WHO'S DRIVING?

A guy was hitchhiking on a very dark night in the middle of a downpour so powerful he could hardly see a few feet ahead.

Suddenly, a car slowly came toward him and stopped.

Blinded by the rain and darkness, he jumped into the back seat, closed the door and then realized there was nobody behind the wheel! The car started moving slowly and then headed straight toward a curve. Scared to death, he started to pray, begging for his life.

Just before the curve, a hand suddenly appeared through the window and moved the wheel. The guy, paralyzed in terror, watched how the hand appeared every time the car approached a curve.

Summoning all his courage, the man jumped out of the car and ran to the nearest town. He stumbled into a restaurant and told everybody what had happened.

It got very quiet when they realized the guy was serious.

About half an hour later, two guys walked into the same restaurant. They were looking for a table when one said, "Look, John, that's the guy who got in the car when we were pushing it."

Can you look back and see where the hand of God has helped steer you in the right direction? Why not let him direct your life every day, starting with today?

Trust in the LORD with all your heart
and lean not on your own understanding;
in all your ways submit to him,
and he will make your paths straight (Proverbs 3:5-6).

OPEN MOUTH, INSERT FOOT

While bicycling with my wife, Diane, I began to cough uncontrollably. I pulled to the side of the road and lay in the grass trying to catch my breath. Finally, with one violent cough a huge beetle tumbled out of my mouth.

When Diane saw what had caused the problem, she began laughing hysterically—after she had killed the prehistoric beast, of course. Between her own gasps for breath she said, "How many times have I told you to keep your mouth shut?"

Of course she was just teasing me, but it's a lesson I am still learning. My first instinct is to correct, to disagree, to judge or to "fix it" with a single sentence. So many relationships are damaged by people who speak before they think or listen.

My dad, a veteran of WWII, used to say, "Loose lips sink ships."

The Scriptures leave no doubt. We need to be careful about what we say.

Set a guard over my mouth, LORD; keep watch over the door of my lips (Psalms 141:3).

A fool speaks without thinking. A closed mouth gathers no foot— or bugs!

PACE YOURSELF

In a long-distance race, it is important to pace yourself. I joined the track team in high school and trained to run 800 meters—about half a mile. On the day of an important track meet, I was ready to go.

This was a special day because my girlfriend was in the stands. I confess, I had never spoken to her, but I wished she was my girlfriend. And winning this race might have attracted her attention and her affection.

When the gun went off, I took off like a shot. After the first turn, I was ahead of everybody. Then, suddenly, I ran out of gas. I tried to keep going, but it was impossible. I had started out too fast.

My stomach sent a message to my brain informing me that the sandwich I had eaten earlier in the day didn't want to run with me anymore.

Before I knew it, I was kneeling on the infield grass. The

sandwich came up first, followed by pizza I had eaten a few days earlier.

Instead of pacing myself and running to finish the race, I tried to beat the others and failed to do either. The race of life isn't about speed, it is about endurance.

The author of Hebrews says, *"Let us run with perseverance the race marked out for us, fixing our eyes on Jesus, the pioneer and perfecter of faith"* (Hebrews 12:1-2).

FROM HUT TO HUT

A man was stranded on the deserted Pacific island for years. One day, a boat sailed into view. The man frantically waved and drew the skipper's attention. The boat anchored near the island and the sailor got out and greeted the marooned man.

After a while the sailor asked, "What are those three huts you have built there?"

The man pointed to the nearest and said, "Well, that's my house there."

"What's that next hut?" asked the sailor.

The man said, "I built that hut to be my church."

The sailor asked, "What about the other hut?"

"Oh, that's where I used to go to church."

Sound familiar?

Many people spend a lifetime hopping from church to church looking for the one that will be perfect. The first time they are offended, meet difficult people, or disagree with the pastor, they begin looking for another hut. If only we could find people just like us.

It's a fruitless search.

Let us consider how we may spur one another on toward love and good deeds, not giving up meeting together, as some are in the habit of doing, but encouraging one another—and all the more as you see the Day approaching (Hebrews 10:24).

Lord, protect me from ever finding a church filled with people just like me. Help me to find a church with people who strive to be like you. Help me to be faithful in attendance and look for every opportunity to love and serve other imperfect people.

THE ALARM BEFORE THE ALARM

You are sound asleep. I'm talking about a ripsnorting, pillow-drooling, dead-to-the-world sleep. Your alarm clock is set to go off at 5 a.m. At precisely 4:55, the clock makes a little click sound.

I don't know why it does this. Maybe the alarm has its own alarm to wake it up so it can wake us up! All I know is that a few minutes before the alarm goes off, it makes that click sound in joyful anticipation of destroying your rest.

That tiny noise makes you sit straight up in bed, wide awake and angry that the click robbed you of five full minutes of sleep. It's no use in going back to sleep because just as you doze off, the big alarm will go off. Does this sound familiar?

Lord, make my heart acutely attuned the still small click of God's voice. Give me the wisdom to listen and courage to respond in such a way that He doesn't have to sound an alarm.

Let me hear what God the LORD will speak,
for he will speak peace to his people, to his saints;
but let them not turn back to folly
(Psalm 85:8, ESV).

GOLF, SANITY AND REPENTANCE

My golf ball had become a water-seeking missile, so I engaged the services of a golf pro to help me keep the ball in the fairway. The first ball I hit arced into a lake to the right of the fairway. "You're too stiff," the pro said. "Wiggle before you swing. It will relax you."

So I wiggled and hit a beautiful soaring shot right into the lake. I got another ball, did the wiggle thing and again the ball went into the lake.

I reasoned, *Surely if I aim at the nice homes on the side of the fairway opposite the lake, the ball will land in the fairway*. I teed up, did the little wiggle, and hit the ball as hard as I could. It hit the inside of my club, then the inside of my heel, and scooted across the grass into the lake.

Someone defined insanity as continuing to do the same thing over and over expecting a different result. I live out that definition every time I step on the golf course.

The Bible has a cure for this kind of insanity; it's called repentance. It means to change direction. God's people sometimes need a dose of sanity.

If my people, who are called by my name, will humble themselves and pray and seek my face and turn from their wicked ways, then I will hear from heaven, and I will forgive their sin and will heal their land (2 Chronicles 7:14).

Is it time for a little sanity in your life?

Go Deeper: 2 Chronicles 7:11-16

A CAN OF WORMS

A minister decided that a visual demonstration would add emphasis to his Sunday sermon. Four worms were placed in four separate jars.

- The first worm was put into a container of alcohol.
- The second worm was put into a container of cigarette smoke.
- The third worm was put into a container of chocolate syrup.
- The fourth worm was put into a container of good clean soil.

At the conclusion of the sermon, the minister reported the following results:

- The first worm in alcohol—dead.
- The second worm in cigarette smoke—dead.
- The third worm in chocolate syrup—dead
- The fourth worm in good clean soil—alive.

So the minister asked the congregation what they could

learn from the demonstration.

An elderly lady was sitting in the back. She quickly raised her hand and said, "As long as you drink, smoke, and eat chocolate, you won't have worms!"

That pretty much ended the service.

That logic is so backward that it's funny. Sadly, people sometimes go to unbelievable lengths to twist the truth to fit their own needs.

Listen to this!

The wrath of God is being revealed from heaven against all the godlessness and wickedness of people, who suppress the truth by their wickedness, since what may be known about God is plain to them, because God has made it plain to them (Romans 1:18-19).

Don't open that can of worms. Jesus said, *"If you hold to my teaching, you are really my disciples. Then you will know the truth, and the truth will set you free" (John 8:31-32).*

THE RIGHT QUESTIONS AND A GENTLE ANSWER

A man lay sprawled across three entire seats in the posh theater. When the usher noticed this, he whispered to the man, "Sorry, sir, but you're only allowed one seat."

The man groaned but didn't budge. The usher became impatient.

"Sir, if you don't get up, I'm going to have to call the manager."

Again, the man just groaned. The infuriated usher marched up the aisle in search of his manager. In a few moments, both the usher and the manager returned and stood over the man. Together the two of them tried to move him, but with no success.

Finally, they summoned the police.

The cop surveyed the situation briefly and then asked, "All right buddy, what's your name?"

"Sam," the man moaned.

"Where are ya from, Sam?"

With pain in his voice Sam replied, "The balcony."

This person didn't need a recitation of rules, and he certainly could not respond to the usher's threats. The right questions, a sympathetic ear, and a gentle response are the ingredients that can lead to a powerful witness.

In your hearts revere Christ as Lord. Always be prepared to give an answer to everyone who asks you to give the reason for the hope that you have. But do this with gentleness and respect (1 Peter 3:15).

GOD IS AT WORK

An older woman went to a walk-in clinic where she was seen by a young, new doctor. After about three minutes in the examination room, the doctor told her she was pregnant.

She burst out the door, screaming as she ran down the hall. An older doctor stopped her and asked what the problem was. She told him what had happened. After listening, he had her sit down and relax in another exam room.

The doctor marched down the hallway to where the young doctor was and demanded, "What's the matter with you? Mrs. Terry is fifty-nine years old, has four grown children and seven grandchildren, and you told her she's pregnant?"

The young doctor continued to write on his clipboard, and without looking up, asked, "Does she still have the hiccups?"

This story reminded me of something I have heard since childhood: "The Lord works in mysterious ways." Too often we respond to any speed bump in life screaming in despair rather than taking a moment to see how God might be using an experience to benefit us.

We know that in all things God works for the good of those who love him, who have been called according to his purpose (Romans 8:28).

When a challenge appears in life, don't run away screaming—relax. Believe that God can use this experience for good. He might be trying to cure a hiccup in your life.

GO DEEPER: ROMANS 8:18-29

IS HE SMOOTH?

A little girl asked her mother, "Can I go outside and play with the boys?"

Her mother replied, "No, you can't play with the boys; they're too rough."

The little girl thought for a few moments and asked, "If I find a smooth one, can I play with him?"

In our home the answer would be, "No, there is no such thing as a smooth boy."

My grandson is a perfect example. He is sweet and bright and can talk you into early retirement, but he is not smooth. After observing three granddaughters who dissolve into tears if their hands get muddy, it has been an interesting adjustment to watch a boy who eats mud for lunch.

I bristle at some of the smooth pictures painted of

Christ. The Bible paints a different picture. This is the man whose hands created and sustains all we see. This is the man who overturned the moneychangers' tables and cast out demons. This is God in the flesh who endured the cross and rose from the dead.

He was rugged, courageous, loving, and compassionate. But He was not smooth.

Therefore God exalted him to the highest place and gave him the name that is above every name, that at the name of Jesus every knee should bow, in heaven and on earth and under the earth, and every tongue acknowledge that Jesus Christ is Lord, to the glory of God the Father (Philippians 2:9-11).

GO DEEPER: PHILIPPIANS 2:1-11

BREAKING THE BLANKIE HABIT

One of the strongest addictions in the universe is the desperate need a child has for a "blankie." You know, that favorite little piece of cloth that is either rubbed on the nose as they suck their thumb, or gummed and sucked into oblivion as they rub their nose?

If you don't believe in the power of blankie addiction, just keep a child overnight when he or she has left blankie at home. No one will sleep that night.

Have you ever smelled a blankie? Unless you enjoy retching uncontrollably, I don't recommend it.

My daughter tried taking her first child's blankie away "cold turkey." It's lucky any of us are still alive. Next time she used an ingenious method. Every three days she cut blankie in half. Within weeks, the child was clutching a tiny, foul-smelling piece of cloth about the size of a large postage stamp. Then one day it was forgotten.

I know adults who have dragged blankies around for years. Today would be a good time to ask God for the strength to cut a blankie habit in half. Tomorrow do it again. Eventually you will be blankie free.

Let us throw off everything that hinders and the sin that so easily entangles. And let us run with perseverance the race marked out for us (Hebrews 12:1).

LISTEN TO GOD

On the way to drop off her daughter at preschool, a doctor left her stethoscope on the car seat. Soon her little girl picked it up and began playing with it.

Be still, my heart, thought the doctor, *my daughter wants to follow in my footsteps!*

Then the child spoke into the instrument: "Welcome to McDonald's. May I take your order?"

A child's thought process is so refreshing. They don't think about how much money they will make, how prestigious their job will be, or what people will think—only about what brings the most joy.

I spent my childhood believing I would be a fireman. In later life I thought seriously about being a doctor. My mom and dad wanted me to be a preacher, so I focused all my studies in that direction and ended up being a comedian/evangelist/motivational speaker. There isn't even a category for what God called me to do.

If you want your daughter to be a doctor, leave your stethoscope on the seat. If you want your child to be a preacher, leave offering plates lying around, but the best way to prepare our children for a life of significance is to teach them to listen to God.

Who they become in Christ will be much more important than what they become.

Hear, O Israel: The LORD our God, the LORD is one. Love the LORD your God with all your heart and with all your soul and with all your strength. These commandments that I give you today are to be on your hearts. Impress them on your children. Talk about them when you sit at home and when you walk along the road, when you lie down and when you get up. Tie them as symbols on your hands and bind them on your foreheads. Write them on the door frames of your houses and on your gates (Deuteronomy 6:4-9).

FINISHING WELL

A man desperate for water was walking through the Sahara desert when he saw something in the distance. Hoping to find water, he walked toward the image only to find a little old woman sitting at a table covered with neckties.

"Please," he begged, "Can I have some water?"

The woman said, "I don't have any water, but why don't you buy a tie? Here's one that goes nicely with your outfit."

The man shouted, "Are you crazy? I don't want a tie, I need water!"

"Okay, don't buy a tie. But I'll still be nice to you. Just four miles over that hill is a restaurant. They'll give you all the water you want."

The dehydrated soul thanked the woman and disappeared over the hill.

Three hours later, he came crawling back.

She said, "I told you, about four miles over that hill is a restaurant. Couldn't you find it?"

The man rasped, "I found it all right. They wouldn't let me in without a tie."

This story reminded me of a message I delivered on finishing well. Finishing well is not about living the last days of life in a godly manner, it is about living each moment in a godly manner. What you do today shapes what you will be tomorrow.

Now is the time to buy the tie and put it on. They don't hand them out at the restaurant— or the finish line.

GO DEEPER: HEBREWS 11

LIVE UP TO YOUR BUMPER STICKER

An impatient man was being tailgated by a stressed-out woman. Suddenly, the light turned yellow just in front of him. He did the right thing and stopped, even though he could have beaten the red light.

The tailgating woman hit the roof and the horn, screaming obscenities because she missed her chance to get through the intersection.

Then she heard a tap on her window and looked up into the face of a serious police officer. The officer ordered her out of the car with her hands up. He took her to the police station, where she was searched, fingerprinted, and placed in a cell.

After a couple of hours, another policeman opened the cell door and escorted her back to the booking desk, where the arresting officer was waiting with her personal effects.

"I'm very sorry for this mistake," he said. "You see, I pulled up behind your car while you were blowing your horn, making obscene gestures, and cussing a blue streak."

"I noticed the 'What Would Jesus Do' bumper sticker, the 'Follow Me to Sunday School' bumper sticker and the chrome-plated Christian fish emblem on the trunk. Naturally, I assumed you had stolen the car."

Ouch!

Our life, not our bumper sticker, is the real testimony of what we believe. We are saved by faith and not by works, but our actions should demonstrate that faith.

What good is it, my brothers and sisters, if someone claims to have faith but has no deeds? Can such faith save them? Suppose a brother or a sister is without clothes and daily food. If one of you says to them, "Go in peace; keep warm and well fed," but does nothing about their physical needs, what good is it? In the same way, faith by itself, if it is not accompanied by action, is dead (James 2:14-17).

THE BEST BATTER IN THE WORLD

A little boy strutted through the backyard, wearing his baseball cap and toting a ball and bat. "I'm the greatest hitter in the world," he said as he tossed the ball into the air, swung at it, and missed. "Strike one!" he yelled.

Undaunted, he picked up the ball and said again, "I'm the greatest hitter in the world!" He tossed the ball into the air and missed again. "Strike two!" he cried.

He examined his bat carefully. Then he spat on his hands, gritted his teeth and yelled, "I'm the greatest hitter in the world!" Again, he tossed the ball up in the air, swung at it—and missed. "Strike three!"

There was a moment of defeat, then his face brightened and he shouted, "Wow! I'm the greatest pitcher in the world!"

What a great attitude, but the story points out an interesting phenomenon in our culture. In our world, self-

esteem is treated as a personal right. Recently, I watched a television program where a prostitute and a murderer proudly proclaimed their actions were justified because they felt good about themselves.

Our self-worth is not determined by what we accomplish or by how we feel about ourselves. Our worth was established on the cross of Christ.

We struck out big time.

All have sinned and fall short of the glory of God (Romans 3:23).

The wages of sin is death (Romans 6:23).

Christ went to bat for us.

But the gift of God is eternal life in Christ Jesus our Lord (Romans 6:23).

Home run!

WHAT DOES GOD LOOK LIKE?

Little Sally was drawing intently when her teacher asked, "What are you drawing?"

"It's a picture of God," Sally answered.

"But no one knows what God looks like," said the teacher.

The little girl looked up said, "They will when I'm finished."

I am intrigued by Sally's certainty of what God looks like. But more than that I am reminded of the Bible's exhortation for us to live like Christ: To have His mind, His compassion, and His love.

I remembered one of my camp counselors telling me that I might be the only glimpse of God that some people will see. I thought through that little story again but from a different perspective.

Ken Davis was intently living his life when someone came up to him and asked, "What are you doing?" To which Ken responded, "I am living my life to be like Jesus." The person challenged, "But no one knows what Jesus was like."

You see where I am going with this?

My prayer is that I will live my life in such a way that I would be able to respond, "They will know what He is like when I am finished." Paul put it this way:

For you were once darkness, but now you are light in the Lord. Live as children of light (Ephesians 5:8).

Will our lives give people a glimpse of what God is like?

SELECTIVE PERCEPTION

"All I see is trouble all around me."

That was the theme of an email I recently received.

I was truly saddened by the circumstances my friend was facing, but I was also reminded of something Mom used to say: "Don't go looking for trouble." That's wise advice because we usually find what we look for.

If we wake up in the morning waiting for something bad to happen, we won't have to wait long. Sadder still, while waiting, God will hand us a dozen blessings we won't see.

It's called selective perception. A person late for an appointment will see every clock on the street. A hungry traveler will see every billboard with food on it. When we are going through difficult times, we sometimes develop ingrown eyeballs disease.

People with ingrown eyeballs only see their own problems. They are blinded to everyday blessings and oblivious to the needs of those around them.

At Lazarus's funeral, Martha had ingrown eyeballs.

When Peter was walking on water, he took his eyes off Jesus and suddenly developed ingrown eyeballs. The fun was over!

Finally, brothers and sisters, whatever is true, whatever is noble, whatever is right, whatever is pure, whatever is lovely, whatever is admirable—if anything is excellent or praiseworthy—think about such things (Philippians 4:8).

Look for good things today. Watch for opportunity to bless someone. You will find what you look for.

WHAT DOES A HERO LOOK LIKE?

While taking a routine vandalism report at an elementary school, a policeman was interrupted by a little girl about six years old. She stared at his uniform and asked, "Are you a cop?"

Without looking up, the policeman said yes and continued writing the report.

The little girl continued, "My mother said if I ever needed help, I should ask the police. Is that right?"

This time he looked at the bright-eyed little girl and said, "Yes, that's right."

The little girl extended her foot and said, "Well, then, would you tie my shoe?"

In that moment, what was the greatest, most heroic thing the man with a uniform and a gun could do?

Kneel down and tie a little girl's shoe.

Real heroes don't wait for monumental, historic moments to act; they practice the characteristics of a hero in the little moments of life. They pause to talk to an elderly man sitting alone in the park, cheer for the last person to cross the finish line, or leave a generous tip for a hard-working waiter.

Look for your moment to be a hero today.

The King will reply, "Truly I tell you, whatever you did for one of the least of these brothers and sisters of mine, you did for me"
(Matthew 25:40).

DON'T JUMP

The owner of a large factory decided to make a surprise visit and check on his workers. Walking through the plant, he noticed a young man leaning lazily against a post. Angrily, he walked up to the young man and said, "Just how much are you being paid a week?"

A bit surprised, the young man responded, "Three hundred dollars."

The owner took out his wallet and counted out three hundred dollars. He slapped the money into the boy's hands and said, "Here's a week's pay—now get out and don't ever come back!" Turning to one of his supervisors, the owner asked, "How long has that lazy bum been working here?"

The supervisor said, "He's not an employee, sir. He was just here to deliver a pizza."

Do you ever jump to conclusions and react in anger? I am tempted to do it all the time. But it is important to

listen and get the complete story before you open your mouth.

What conclusion do you jump to when you see a teen with piercings and tattoos skateboard down the street? What assumption do you make when you see a well-dressed man step out of a limousine?

James 1:19-20 says, *"My dear brothers and sisters, take note of this: Everyone should be quick to listen, slow to speak and slow to become angry, because human anger does not produce the righteousness that God desires."*

Don't jump to conclusions! Listen and reach out! Beneath the outward appearance, you may discover a heart that needs to know the love of God.

You might also save three hundred dollars.

BEING EMOTIONAL WITH GOD

Men aren't known to be very good at expressing emotion. Maybe it's a dysfunction we have learned from modern culture. A man would never come home and sob, "Honey, today I felt a hurt deep down in my stomach. As the day went on it moved up into my heart, and then suddenly tears began to flow. . . and then . . . then . . . I started to eat chocolate."

Men don't express their feelings that way. They tend to withdraw, get grumpy, and kick the cat. Cats always know when a man has "feelings."

But perhaps men have something to learn from women. Certainly we have something to learn from God.

King David had no problem crying out to God in anguish, and God called him a man after His own heart. Jeremiah was known as the weeping prophet.

Maybe we strong, silent types aren't as strong as we think. Is it possible that hiding our feelings keeps us from openness with God?

The righteous cry out, and the LORD hears them;
he delivers them from all their troubles.
The LORD is close to the brokenhearted
and saves those who are crushed in spirit (Psalm 34:17-18).

I'm not saying we need to start wailing uncontrollably in public, but it might be time for some of us to let go of pent-up emotions and let God do a miracle. At least the cat will be grateful!

Lord, you know all there is to know about me and still you love me. Give me the confidence to cry out to you and experience your deliverance.

MICROPHOBIAS

After years of riding in our private plane, my wife announced, "I am starting to fear flying."

I queried, "Why would you be afraid? I'm the pilot."

She was silent. So much for her confidence in my piloting skills.

Then she blurted, "I am afraid of small planes."

This kind of reasoning kills me. Nobody's afraid of small things! Little kids don't come out of their bedrooms and say, "I think there's a microscopic creature under my bed," or "Daddy, there's a tiny monster in the closet." It's the *big*, giant, hairy stuff that's scary!

Women never go into stores and say, "Bring me a humongous pair of shoes! I'm afraid of small shoes."

It turns out, there is a term for people who are afraid of small things. They're called microphobics. There are terms for other fears as well. Anthophobia is the fear of flowers. Autodysomophobia is the fear of one's own body odor. If you're afraid of long words, you have sesquipedalophobia. Talk about cruel irony—that may be the longest word I have ever seen!

Hebrews 13:6 says, "The Lord is my helper; I will not be afraid."

Fear of any kind is paralyzing. Counseling helps, but it is the love of God that drives out fear.

There is no fear in love. But perfect love drives out fear, because fear has to do with punishment. The one who fears is not made perfect in love (1 John 4:18).

Go Deeper: Psalm 91

41

HAUNTED BY A COW

In 2008, after hitting a two-thousand-pound cow at seventy miles an hour, I tried to get the insurance company to give us a new car. They said, "No, we'll fix this one."

I said, "Excuse me, the engine is sitting in the front seat and there's cow hair in the trunk. Total the car!"

"No, we'll fix it."

Modern cars are merely a computer shrouded by metal. In my humble opinion, nothing hurts a computer more than a seventy-mile-an-hour encounter with a two thousand pound cow. Ya can't fix that!

When we got the "fixed" car back, it looked great on the outside, but the computer had PTCID (Post-Traumatic Cow Impact Disorder). The car thermometer would read -63°F even though it was actually 100°F outside. To compensate, the confused computer would turn on the heater, and we would abandon the car.

I think the car was haunted by the cow. Sometimes, when it was quiet, I could hear a mournful "moo" coming from the trunk.

Computers are marvelous, complicated machines. When they break, it takes an expert to fix them. You are a million times more marvelous than any computer. If your life feels like you've hit a two-thousand-pound cow, don't try to fix it on your own. Total it! Give it all to *the* expert. Let Him make you new.

If anyone is in Christ, that person is a new creation: The old has gone, the new is here! All this is from God, who reconciled us to himself through Christ and gave us the ministry of reconciliation (2 Corinthians 5:17-18).

GO DEEPER: 2 CORINTHIANS 5

THE INHERITANCE

A wealthy old man looked around the table at his two sons, five daughters, and their spouses, who were gathered for a family reunion.

"Not a single grandchild," he said with a sigh. "Why, I'll give a million dollars to the first person who presents me with a little one. Now, let's say a blessing for this food." He then bowed his head and prayed.

When the old man lifted his head, his wife was the only one still sitting at the table.

Down through history men and women have cajoled, connived, and even committed murder in an attempt to gain an inheritance. One man waited for years to receive his inheritance only to discover his mother left everything to her cat!

Do you long for an inheritance? Listen to this!

Praise be to the God and Father of our Lord Jesus Christ! In his great mercy he has given us new birth into a living hope through the resurrection of Jesus Christ from the dead, and into an inheritance that can never perish, spoil or fade. This inheritance is kept in heaven for you, who through faith are shielded by God's power until the coming of the salvation that is ready to be revealed in the last time (1 Peter 1:3-5).

We praise you, Father, that our inheritance is worth more than gold. Thank you that it has been reserved for us for eternity.

DEATH AND TAXES

Have you ever noticed that when you put the two words *the* and *IRS* together it spells "theirs"?

Ever since the establishment of the first government, people have been fighting for a simplified tax return. We should be careful what we ask for. If the government has it's way, there will only be two lines in the new document:

How much did you make?

Send it in.

Benjamin Franklin said, "In this world nothing can be said to be certain, except death and taxes."

Actually, there is much more we can be sure of. Neither death nor taxes can rob us of what is most important in life.

The teachers of the law tried to trick Jesus by asking, "Is it right for us to pay taxes to Caesar?"

His answer astonished them: "Give back to Caesar what is Caesar's, and to God what is God's."

Caesar's agenda flew in the face of the morals and ideals of God's people. It must have been hard to pay taxes to such a government. But Jesus knew that true riches lie somewhere else.

Money is a temporary means of exchange established by the government. You can be sure every government will take some of it. Our salvation, however, was purchased with a currency of far greater value: the blood of Christ. We belong to God. Nothing can take away what He has given us.

I am convinced that neither death nor life, neither angels nor demons, neither the present nor the future, nor any powers, neither height nor depth, nor anything else in all creation, will be able to separate us from the love of God that is in Christ Jesus our Lord (Romans 8:38-39).

Lord help me give back to you what you have given me—my life!

SUPER SHEEP

When I read that the Bible compares us to sheep, I was upset. It's true we get into trouble like sheep do, but sheep are chicken—afraid of their own shadow.

We had a horse named Lightning who used to kill sheep. It wasn't premeditated. He didn't sit in his stall and plot wooly homicide: *I'm going to kill me a sheep.* Instead, he would see sheep running across the pasture and think, *Whoa! It's a Nerf ball!* And the chase was on.

Lightning would chase the whole flock, and then with a swoop of his neck tip one over! Occasionally, a sheep would die, not because the horse hurt him, but because he was scared right out of his wool. I could see the look of fear on the sheep's face: *Oh no . . . I've been tipped over.* And he'd die.

Sheep are just plain chicken.

Throughout the Bible, God's children are compared to sheep. We most certainly were created to follow our Shepherd and listen for His voice, but to our own detriment, we skitter around following each other.

Though we are like sheep, God never intended for us to live like soft, timid creatures who roll over and die at the slightest provocation!

God told Joshua, *"Be strong and courageous. Do not be afraid; do not be discouraged, for the LORD your God will be with you wherever you go" (Joshua 1:9).*

I've never read a verse that explains what to do when a horse tips us over, but when the storms of life upset us, God gives His sheep the strength and courage to stand up and be baaaaad.

GO DEEPER: EPHESIANS 6:10-17

AN IMPATIENT PATIENT

I woke up one morning with a sinus infection. There was a lump above my right eye the size of a golf ball. The pain was so intense I couldn't open that eye, and tears were shooting out of my other eye. So, blind in my right eye and unable to see out of my left, I drove fifteen miles to the clinic.

When I got there, the waiting room was crammed with sniffling, coughing people. I sat for over an hour absorbing the germs of strangers. Hanging in one corner was an ornamental skeleton. I wondered how long he had been waiting.

In our impatient culture, waiting is unbearable. However, patience is listed as one of the fruits of the Spirit (see Galatians 5:22-23). Although we might contract an illness waiting for the doctor, there are definite benefits for those who are willing to wait on the Lord.

They who wait for the LORD shall renew their strength;
they shall mount up with wings like eagles;
they shall run and not be weary;
they shall walk and not faint (Isaiah 40:31, ESV).

That is something worth waiting for!

Lord, too many times I struggle to fly without you. Help me wait for your word, your timing, and your strength. Be the wind beneath my wings. Help me soar!

LET IT GO

While hiking, a man stumbled and slid over a precipice. He grabbed a branch protruding from the side of the cliff. He could not climb back up, below him lay certain death, and he was slowly losing his grip on the branch.

In desperation the man began to scream: "Help! Is anybody up there?"

To his amazement, a booming voice answered: "I am here. I am God, and I will help you." The man yelled, "Throw down a rope."

"I don't have a rope," God responded, "but I can help you if you trust me."

By now the man could barely hang on. "I trust you," he screamed.

God's voice boomed, "Then let go of the branch!"

There was a moment of silence, and then the man yelled again, "Is anybody else up there?"

The answer to that question is no! God is our only hope. So often we are unwilling to trust Him. Instead, we cling to something that cannot save us. We have our own rescue plan. Our grip is weak and the branch is giving way, but we hang on for dear life.

If you want dear life, follow this advice:

Trust in the LORD with all your heart
and lean not on your own understanding;
In all your ways submit to him,
and he will make your paths straight
(Proverbs 3:5-6).

Lord help me let go and let you show me your saving power.

ANOTHER NIGHT WITH THE FROGS

A fascinating story is found in the book of Exodus. Because of Pharaoh's stubbornness, God sends a plague of frogs upon Egypt. The country has already suffered a plague in which every drop of the Nile River turned to blood, yet Pharaoh hardens his heart toward God and refuses to set the children of Israel free.

So Moses stretches forth his hand and a plague of frogs appears. Frogs are everywhere. They are in the people's beds, in their food, even in the driveway. Hundreds are killed every time Pharaoh backs the chariot out of the garage.

When Moses offers to rid Egypt of the frogs, Pharaoh gives a bizarre response. He says, "Do it tomorrow." He chooses to spend another night with the frogs rather than obey God. I'm pretty sure he didn't consult his wife on that decision.

It's easy to accuse Pharaoh of stupidity, yet how many times do we ignore God in much the same way. He reveals the steps that will free us from the bondage of a bad attitude or destructive habit. Our response? *Maybe tomorrow. Give me a couple of days. I can do this my way.*

To such a response, Scripture has a stern warning:

Today, if you hear his voice,
do not harden your hearts (Hebrews 4:7).

Don't spend another night with the frogs. Let God deliver you today!

GO DEEPER: EXODUS 8

BACK TO LIFE

A lady looked out the window of her home one day and was horrified to see her German shepherd shaking the life out of the neighbor's rabbit. She knew this was going to cause friction with the neighbor, so she grabbed a broom, ran outside, and beat the dog until he dropped the rabbit, which was now covered in dog spit and extremely dead.

She made sure no one was looking, carefully scooped up the rabbit on the end of the broom, and brought it into the house. Once there, she dumped the rabbit into the bathtub, turned on the shower, and directed the spray at the lifeless body until it was clean. Then she grabbed her hair drier and blew the bunny dry. He looked pretty good. Almost alive.

When the neighbor wasn't watching, the lady climbed over the fence and propped the rabbit upright in its cage.

About an hour later, she heard screams coming from the neighbor's yard. "What's happened?" she asked, pretending she didn't know.

The neighbor came running to the fence—pale and trembling. "It's our rabbit! He died two weeks ago, so we buried him," she sobbed. "Now he's back!"

Unfortunately, instead of living fully alive, we exist like dead fluffed-up rabbits, working hard to keep the appearance of life on the outside while on the inside we feel like we are dying.

Irenaeus of Lyons said, *"The glory of God is man fully alive." Jesus said, "I have come that they may have life, and have it to the full"* (John 10:10).

God has given us eternal and abundant life. It starts the day we trust in Jesus. Today can be the day we stop leaning against the cage. Hop to it! Lighten up and live.

Go Deeper: Ephesians 5:8-20

BODY COUNTS

I have two beautiful daughters who could take hours getting ready for school. Their outward appearance was of utmost importance to them.

Not a hair could be out of place; not an eyebrow could go unattended. The floor in their bathroom was so sticky from hairspray that small bugs got stuck and perished there.

However, when it came to the appearance of their rooms, they lived like pigs. One day I saw mice and roaches scurrying away with their little suitcases and squeaking, "We can't live like this any more!"

Our bodies are an important part of life, and it is important to take care of them. After all, we are created in the image of a magnificent God, and the Bible says our bodies are temples of the Holy Spirit.

My daughters spent hours beautifying the Holy Spirit's house. I wish they had been a little more concerned about cleaning up mine.

This reminds me that *"The LORD does not look at the things people look at. People look at the outward appearance, but the LORD looks at the heart"* *(1Samuel 16:7).*

Lord, my heart is your home. Help me keep it presentable in your sight. I want you to feel welcome here.

NO SUCH THING AS SWEET REVENGE

A man and his wife were in their house listening to the neighbor's dog, who had been barking incessantly for hours.

Finally, the man jumped up and said, "I've had enough of this!"

He rushed downstairs and disappeared. Quite a bit of time passed before he finally returned.

He sat down without saying a word. Finally, the wife said, "The dog is still barking, What did you do while you were gone?"

The man replied, "I put the dog in our backyard. Now, let's see how they like it!"

Did you know that an unforgiving, vengeful spirit is deadly? Not to the person it is directed at but to the person who holds it. As someone once said, "Bitterness is like drinking poison and waiting for the other person to die."[1]

Do not repay anyone evil for evil. Be careful to do what is right in the eyes of everyone. If it is possible, as far as it depends on you, live at peace with everyone. Do not take revenge, my dear friends, but leave room for God's wrath, for it is written: "It is mine to avenge; I will repay," says the Lord (Romans 12:17-19).

Don't let a spirit of revenge destroy you. Ask God for the strength to forgive. It will enable you to lighten up and live.

GO DEEPER: ROMANS 12:17-21

---

[1]See Joanna Weaver, *Having a Mary Spirit: Allowing God to Change Us from the Inside Out* (Colorado Springs: WaterBrook, 2006), p. 153.

NO EXCUSES

Here are some notes written by parents requesting that their children be excused from school. The misspelled words made the teacher's day.

"My son is under a doctor's care and should not take physical education today. Please execute him."

A little girl's slip read, "Please excuse Lisa for being absent. She was sick and I had her shot."

I love this one. "Megan could not come to school today because she has been bothered by very close veins."

How about this plea? "Please excuse Jennifer for missing school yesterday. We forgot to get the Sunday paper off the porch, and when we found it Monday, we thought it was Sunday."

When God called Moses to go to Pharaoh and demand that he set the Hebrew people free, Moses responded, "Who am I that I should go to Pharaoh and bring the Israelites out of Egypt?" God's answer: "I will be with you."

This wasn't good enough for Moses. He tried every excuse in the book to avoid God's call:

- I don't have enough influence.
- I don't know what to say.
- What if they don't believe me.
- I'm not a good speaker.

Finally, Moses asked God to send somebody else. But God never calls anyone to a task without first perfectly equipping that person for the task. In spite of his protests, Moses became one of the greatest prophets ever.

Since then, no prophet has risen in Israel like Moses, whom the LORD knew face to face, who did all those signs and wonders the LORD sent him to do in Egypt—to Pharaoh and to all his officials and to his whole land. For no one has ever shown the mighty power or performed the awesome deeds that Moses did in the sight of all Israel (Deuteronomy 34:10-12).

What is it that God wants you to do? When God calls, there are no excuses.

GO DEEPER: EXODUS 3:7–4:17

BUT DUST?

Every year the *Washington Post* runs a contest where people supply alternate meanings for common words. The following are a few winners from a recent contest.[2]

Coffee: a noun meaning the person upon whom one coughs.

Flabbergasted: an adjective that means appalled over how much weight you have gained.

Negligent: an adjective that describes a condition in which you absent-mindedly answer the door in your nightgown.

Lymph: to walk with a lisp. (I guess then that "lymph node" would mean you are aware that you walk with a lisp.)

Sometimes children misunderstand word meanings and in the process come close to the truth.

In a sermon on grace, the pastor proclaimed that if it were not for the grace of God we would be but dust. A little girl in the congregation turned to her mother and in a voice loud enough for the whole church to hear asked, "What is butt dust?"

I would tell the little girl, "That is the dust that collects when we refuse to get off our backsides and do what God is asking us to do."

Do not merely listen to the word, and so deceive yourselves. Do what it says (James 1:22).

Lord help me be dust free today.

[2]See "WPM Invitational," Washington Post, www.washingtonpostsmensainvitational.com.

BASEBALL IN HEAVEN

Two ninety-year-old men, Bill and Joe, had been friends all of their lives. When it was clear that Joe was dying, Bill visited him every day. One day Bill said, "Joe, we both loved baseball all our lives. Please do me one favor: when you get to heaven, let me know if there's baseball there."

Joe looked up at Bill and said, "You've been my best friend for many years. If it's at all possible, I'll do this favor for you." Shortly after that, Joe died.

At midnight a couple of nights later, Bill was awakened by a blinding flash of white light and a voice calling out to him, "Bill, Bill!"

Bill sat up! "Who is it?"

"Bill, it's me, Joe." I'm in heaven and I'm keeping my promise. I have some really good news and a little bad news."

"Tell me the good news first," said Bill.

Joe said, "The good news is that there is baseball in heaven. All of our old buddies are here. Better than that, we're all young again. Better still, it never rains or snows, and we can play baseball all we want; we never get tired."

"That's fantastic," said Bill. "It's beyond my wildest dreams! So what's the bad news?"

"You're pitching Tuesday."

If you've trusted Christ and are going to heaven, that's good news whether you're pitching or not.

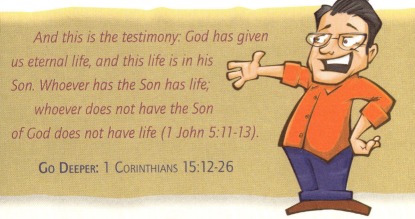

And this is the testimony: God has given us eternal life, and this life is in his Son. Whoever has the Son has life; whoever does not have the Son of God does not have life (1 John 5:11-13).

Go Deeper: 1 Corinthians 15:12-26

EXERCISING FAITH

I heard of a new exercise program that will help you gain strength and stamina.

Begin by standing on a comfortable surface, where you have plenty of room at each side. With a 5 lb. potato sack in each hand, extend your arms straight out from your sides and hold them there as long as you can. Try to reach a full minute, and then relax.

Each day, you'll find that you can hold this position just a bit longer.

After a couple of weeks, move up to 10 lb. potato sacks.

Then try 50 lb. potato sacks. Finally, try to get to where you can lift a 100 lb. potato sack in each hand and hold your arms straight for more than a full minute.

After you feel confident at that level, put a potato in each of the sacks.

Such an anemic plan can't help develop physical or spiritual strength. Physical strength comes from lifting heavy weights. Spiritual strength comes from trusting God with heavy weights.

Ephesians 6:10 encourages us to get in tiptop spiritual shape: *"Be strong in the Lord and in his mighty power."*

Load up those potatoes. Flex your faith muscles today.

GO DEEPER: EPHESIANS 6:10-18

READY, AIM, LIVE!

The first time my dad took me hunting was an unexpected adventure. Shortly after stepping into the forest, a shot rang out. The bullet hit a tree inches from my face.

I took a few more steps and heard another shot. This time the bullet buzzed above my head.

The bullet from the third shot passed so close to my ear that it left me briefly deaf in that ear.

It dawned on me: *Someone is shooting at me!* I dove for the ground as a hail of bullets buzzed past me. My friends began yelling for the man to stop shooting, and thankfully he did.

This man did not choose a target. He was shooting in the direction of sounds he heard, hoping one of his bullets might hit something. One almost hit me! I don't think that was what he had in mind.

Hunters who aim at nothing are dangerous and ineffective. Likewise, those who live without a purpose in life miss the mark of what life is all about. Aim at nothing and you will hit it every time.

Do you have a purpose for living that goes beyond just surviving?

Paul said, *"Forgetting what is behind and straining toward what is ahead, I press on toward the goal to win the prize for which God has called me heavenward in Christ Jesus" (Philippians 3:13-14).*

That's good aim.

BREATHE

While waiting for the airplane to take off, a friendly flight attendant demonstrated the proper use of the oxygen system. "If the cabin should lose pressure," she said, "an oxygen mask will fall from the compartment above you. Grab the mask and pull it toward you. Place the mask over your nose and mouth, tighten the straps, and breathe normally."

Breath *normally*? Are you kidding me?

I would scream for my mother, grab every mask within reach, and suck down enough oxygen for eight people.

Isn't that the way we often respond to sudden emergencies in life? Although God has briefed us about what to do, and promised to supply our every need, we still end up gasping for breath, grabbing for security in all the wrong directions and forgetting His promises.

Here is His briefing again, just in case you need it today.

Do not be anxious about anything, but in every situation, by prayer and petition, with thanksgiving, present your requests to God. And the peace of God, which transcends all understanding, will guard your hearts and your minds in Christ Jesus (Philippians 4:6-7).

Lord, help me take a deep breath and trust your promises today.

WHAT GOES UP...

A "tender" is a small boat that takes passengers from a cruise ship to shore. We were riding one of these boats in very rough seas. As usual, I was acting more like I was five than sixty-five. In the middle of an impromptu dance, I jumped into the air just as the boat crested the top of a large wave.

The boat dropped into a fifteen-foot trough, and I floated in mid-air for about a second before crashing to the deck. I was reminded of the old saying, "What goes up must come down." *Hard!* I must have looked like a dying fish as I flopped in pain on the bottom of the boat.

Later that day, I talked with a man who said he felt like a dying fish. His life was filled with ups and downs. He had experienced business failure and difficulty in his marriage, and he was disappointed with life. I reminded him of our experience on the boat. Life often alternates between periods where we are giddy with weightlessness and then flat on our faces on the bottom of the boat.

Don't despair! Those ups and downs are part of life. Just before He was crucified, Jesus told His disciples, *"In this world you will have trouble. But take heart! I have overcome the world"* (John 16:33).

When you hit bottom, look up. He is the one who will give you the strength to lighten up and live.

SERMON ON MOUNTAIN DRIVING

Author and comedian Bob Stromberg memorized the entire "Sermon on the Mount" from a modern paraphrase called *The Message*. Not long after, he was asked to preach in his father's church. *What a great idea*, he thought. *I will recite the Sermon on the Mount and let that be the sermon*.

On Sunday he recited the passage with the passion he felt Christ might have used. Other than that, he added nothing and left nothing out. After the service several people came up to tell Bob how some part of this message had moved them deeply.

Bob was feeling quite satisfied when an elderly lady added her commentary to the response. After thanking Bob for the wonderful message, she pulled him close and whispered, "Next time, if there is any way you can add something about the way people around here drive, I personally would appreciate it."

Bless her heart. How often do we read Scripture or hear a message and immediately see how it might apply to someone else? But keeping our own heart open for how God's Word might apply to us is the key to spiritual growth.

For the word of God is alive and active. Sharper than any double-edged sword, it penetrates even to dividing soul and spirit, joints and marrow; it judges the thoughts and attitudes of the heart (Hebrews 4:12).

Lord, keep me from swinging the sword of your Word at others. Help me listen for how your Word can change my life.

PEER PRESSURE

Reporters asked a 104-year-old woman, "What do you think is the best thing about being 104?" After a moment's thought, the woman said, "No peer pressure."

Imagine a life without peer pressure! In grade school I remember being pressured to eat glue. We didn't sniff glue back then, we ate it—a thick white paste that tasted like powdered horse hooves with a little sugar mixed in.

In the teen years, peer pressure is like a disease. I remember vividly being pressured by friends to bully a classmate. The pressure to make moral compromises in adolescence is constant and intense.

Unfortunately, peer pressure doesn't end with the onset of adulthood. It just comes from different directions. The pressures of materialism, neglecting the ones we love to pursue success, creative tax preparation, and apathetic Christian living are added to some of the same pressures we faced as teenagers.

Paul challenged us to resist peer pressure by giving everything to Christ, and refusing to "let the world squeeze us into its mold."[3]

Do not conform to the pattern of this world, but be transformed by the renewing of your mind. Then you will be able to test and approve what God's will is—his good, pleasing and perfect will (Romans 12:1-2).

You don't have to wait till your 104 to successfully face peer pressure. That's good news!

[3]See Romans 12:1-2 in the J. B. Phillips Translation.

PATIENCE

Paul wrote, "When the Holy Spirit controls our lives he will produce this kind of fruit in us: love, joy, peace, patience, kindness, goodness, faithfulness, gentleness and self-control" (Galatians 5:22-23, TLB).

What's with the patience thing?

I confess I am not a very patient person. When computers first came out, I would log on to a website and go have a cup of coffee or build an orphanage while I was waiting for a page to download.

Now if a webpage takes more than three seconds to appear, I begin to grumble about the incompetent person who built the thing. Not long ago we had to find a phone and put money into a slot to make a call. Today, we carry tiny phones with us and lose patience immediately if we experience a poor connection.

I think God values patience because it is a sign of unselfishness. We are impatient when we believe the world revolves around us and don't think it's revolving fast enough to meet our needs. Not very godly is it?

So today I prayed, Lord give me patience *and give it to me now!* Looks like I still need help. How about you?

WHAT IFS

When I was a boy, we had pre-air-conditioning features on our car called "wings": little vertical windows that directed outside air into the car. Open the wing and air would hit the glass and fly into the car.

The downside was that the wing also directed anything that was flying in the air into the car.

One Sunday a bee hit the wing, was jettisoned into the car, and got caught in my sweater. I began screaming, "A bee! Agh! Mom! It's a bee! I'm gonna die!"

"Pipe down!" my sympathetic mom shouted." If you don't bother the bee, it won't bother you."

I didn't know what bothered a bee. What if the bee didn't want to go to church? Certainly any bee that just hit a piece of glass at 60 mph would be bothered already.

The "what ifs" of life often paralyze us. What if the

stock market crashes? What if I lose my job? Here's what the Bible says about that kind of worry.

Therefore I tell you, do not worry about your life, what you will eat or drink; or about your body, what you will wear. Is not life more than food, and the body more than clothes? Look at the birds of the air; they do not sow or reap or store away in barns, and yet your heavenly Father feeds them. Are you not much more valuable than they? Can any one of you by worrying add a single hour to your life? (Matthew 6:25-27)

In verse 33, God give the best antidote to worry: *"Seek first his kingdom and his righteousness, and all these things will be given to you as well."*

Wondering what happened to the bee? I killed it with my Bible.

BETTER THAN A SIX-PACK

After suffering the consequences of being overweight and then regaining my health, I wrote a book encouraging people around the world take care of their bodies and live fully alive. In the book, I detailed the discipline it took to regain my physical and spiritual health.[4]

In the beginning, I was intimidated because I compared myself to my friend in California who has muscles in places where I haven't even got places.

He has a six-pack. That's a row of muscles down each side of the abdomen that look like a stack of tiny dinner rolls. During the filming of *Fully Alive* I announced that I had lost 40 lbs. Someone asked if I had a six-pack. The answer is no. I have what looks vaguely like venetian blinds. You don't want to see it!

The point is this: Keeping physically healthy is about much more than vanity. An Army recruiting poster put it this way: "Be all that you can be."

[4]Ken Davis, Fully Alive (Nashville: Thomas Nelson, 2012).

The apostle Paul expressed it another way. *"I want to know Christ—yes, to know the power of his resurrection" (Philippians 3:10).* Paul knew that physical strength without spiritual strength is useless: *"Physical training is of some value, but godliness has value for all things, holding promise for both the present life and the life to come" (1 Timothy 4:8).*

Emotionally, physically, and spiritually, we should strive to be ready for anything God calls us to do. In Christ we have a resource greater than any gym membership. The power that allowed Christ to walk from the grave is available to help us face whatever comes our way today.

Lord, help me know you better. Let me experience the power of your resurrection!

GOD SEES EVERYTHING

A kindergarten teacher handed out a coloring page to her class. On it was a picture of a duck holding an umbrella. The teacher told her class to color the duck yellow and the umbrella green.

But little Johnny, who always did things his way, colored the duck a bright fire-engine red.

After seeing this, the teacher said, "Johnny, how many times have you seen a red duck?"

Without looking up, Johnny replied, "The same number of times I've seen a yellow duck holding an umbrella."

Johnny was no doubt a creative little boy, and my guess would be that he would go far in life. Many of us don't take the time or look close enough to see the obvious things in life.

As a pilot, I am required to inspect my airplane before every takeoff. On one occasion, I walked around the airplane to assure that everything was in working order as I had done hundreds of times before. Then I climbed into the pilot seat and started the plane.

Out of the corner of my eye, I saw a man running toward me waving his arms. I shut the engine down and climbed down from the cockpit.

"You have a flat tire," he said, pointing to my totally deflated front tire. Obviously I had looked without seeing.

I love the fact that God sees everything, even red ducks and the innermost thoughts of our heart. By the way, Johnny, I don't think I have ever seen either a red duck or a yellow duck.

Nothing in all creation is hidden from God's sight. Everything is uncovered and laid bare before the eyes of him to whom we must give account (Hebrews 4:13).

YELLOW LIGHTS AND BLESSINGS

A motorcycle policeman pulled over a car that had just rushed through a yellow light. The driver explained that when the light turned yellow he thought it would be better to speed through than to stop suddenly and risk getting hit from behind. He reminded the officer that it was not illegal to go through a yellow light.

The policeman didn't buy it. He gruffly insisted there was no excuse to speed through a yellow light. "The next time a light turns yellow, you stop!" he snapped. The driver tried once more to explain his fear of being hit from behind, but the policeman cut him off and wrote a warning ticket for reckless driving.

About five blocks later, still fuming over the brusque lecture he had received, the driver approached an intersection just as the light turned yellow. He slammed on the brakes only to hear the squeal of tires and a thump from behind.

The sight he saw in his rearview mirror made up for a rough beginning to the day. The motorcycle policeman was pushing his bike back from the bumper of the car, staring into the distance as though nothing had happened.

Sometimes God uses unique circumstances to bring a smile of blessing to our face. Watch for your blessing today, and be careful at those yellow lights.

Judge not the Lord by feeble sense,
But trust him for his grace,
Behind a frowning providence,
He hides a smiling face.[5]

[5]William Cowper, "God Moves in Mysterious Ways," 1774.

TRUE LOVE HAS 20/20 VISION

Remember the old saying "If you love something, set it free. If it's really yours it will return to you"? Blah, blah, blah. I think I found a more accurate rendition of that strange proverb. The author is unknown but it goes like this:

If you love something, set it free.
If it comes back, it was, and always will be yours.
If it never returns, it was never yours to begin with.
If it just sits in your living room, messes up your stuff, eats your food, uses your telephone, takes your money, and never behaves as if you actually set it free in the first place—you either married it or gave birth to it.[6]

We've all heard the saying "Love is blind." It's a lie. Lust is blind. True love has its eyes wide open. The kind of love that lasts has perfect 20/20 vision. True love sees all the imperfections, missing cookies, messy rooms, and dirty underwear. It sees warts and moles, and loves in spite of it all.

[6] "Set It Free," Funscrape.com, www.funscrape.com/Jokes/Love_Jokes.html.

Love may be blind, but marriage is a real eye-opener. That's right! It's only when your eyes are open that you get the real chance to love. God misses nothing. He sees into the darkest corners of our life and loves us anyway. Then He asks us to love each other in that same way.

God demonstrates his own love for us in this: While we were still sinners, Christ died for us (Romans 5:8).

As I have loved you, so you must love one another (John 13:34).

A SENSITIVE MAN

The room was full of pregnant women and their husbands. The class instructor said, "Ladies, remember that exercise is good for you. And walking is especially beneficial. It strengthens your muscles and will make delivery that much easier. Just pace yourself, make plenty of stops and try to do your walking on a soft grass surface or a path."

Then the instructor spoke to the men. "Gentlemen, remember—you and your wife are in this together. It wouldn't hurt you to walk with her. In fact, that shared experience would be good for you both."

The room became very quiet as the men absorbed this information. After a few moments, a man at the back of the room slowly raised his hand. When the instructor called on him, the man spoke in slow measured tones. "I was just wondering. Would it be all right if she carries a golf bag while we walk?"

It brings a tear to your eye, doesn't it? We men are not always wired for sensitivity. Yet God clearly asks all of us to consider others before ourselves.

Do nothing out of selfish ambition or vain conceit. Rather, in humility value others above yourselves, not looking to your own interests but each of you to the interests of the others (Philippians 2:3-4).

I hope this man survived long enough to learn the lesson.

Go Deeper: Philippians 2

FORGET ABOUT IT

As I'm getting older, I notice that weird things are happening to me. My belly is hanging out, my bones hurt, and I can't remember anything anymore. I walk into a room and make little circles like a dog looking for a place to lie down 'cause I can't remember why I came into the room. Do you ever do that? Do you ever leave the room and come back hoping that will trigger your memory?

I've always had a photographic memory, but evidently I ran out of film. I started recording my thoughts on my cell phone, but I would forget the idea before I could get the phone out of my pocket.

On more than one occasion, I pressed the wrong button on the phone, unknowingly called a friend and dictated my thoughts to him. I can't imagine what my friend thought when he answered the phone and heard me say, "Check the Internet to see how to get rid of carbuncles."

I do think my forgetfulness has its plus side. It helps me in my relationship with my wife. I can't remember what she did that made me angry.

A person's wisdom yields patience;
it is to one's glory to overlook an offense (Proverbs 19:11).

Wise people forget on purpose. It comes naturally to us older folks.

Dear Lord help me today to remember that you forgot my sins. Give me the wisdom and strength to forget and forgive.

LOOK FOR THE RAINBOW

Remember the best-selling booklet *All I Really Need to Know I Learned in Kindergarten*? It had great suggestions like "Take a nap every day," "Don't eat glue"—stuff like that. Well, here's a new one my friend Mikey sent to me: *All I Really Need to Know I Learned from Noah's Ark*.

- Plan ahead. It wasn't raining when Noah built the ark.
- Stay fit. When you're 600 years old, someone might ask you to do something really big.
- Don't listen to critics—do what has to be done.
- Build on high ground. (Boy, that's a good one.)
- Speed isn't always an advantage. The cheetahs were on board, but so were the snails.
- Don't forget that we're all in the same boat.
- When the doo-doo gets really deep, don't sit there and complain—shovel.
- Remember that the ark was built by amateurs and the Titanic was built by professionals.
- If you have to start over, have a friend by your side.
- Remember, woodpeckers inside the boat are a bigger threat than the storm outside.
- Don't miss the boat.

And my favorite lesson to be learned from Noah's ark? No matter how dark the storm, don't give up. Wait for the rainbow!

> *Whenever the rainbow appears in the clouds, I will see it and remember the everlasting covenant between God and all living creatures of every kind on the earth (Genesis 9:16).*
>
> Look for your rainbow today. Lighten up and live.
>
> **GO DEEPER:** GENESIS 8–9

THE GIFT OF EACH OTHER

The inane inconsistency of the politically correct never ceases to amaze me. They argue that there is no difference between men and women, and in the same breath encourage us to celebrate our differences.

I have been married for forty-five years. After that many years, if a person doesn't recognize the differences between men and women they may need a brain scan. God created us equal. But women are smarter.

Here is a list of six differences between men and women I have observed. Note: God makes wonderful exceptions.

- Women look at a cat's facial expressions and say, "Look he's lonely and needs some love." To a man he just looks evil.
- Woman want to talk about feelings; men don't have any!
- Women comparison shop. If a man can find it, he buys it.

- Taking a car trip without trying to beat your best time. Why even go?
- Women know the difference between beige, off-white, and eggshell. Men know that teal is a certain kind of duck.
- Women care about the inaccuracy of the bathroom scale. A man is satisfied as long as the scale is accurate to within 10 lbs!

Thank you, Lord, for making us different, loving us equally, and giving us to each other.

ALL WE LIKE . . . SHEEP?

I was upset when I first discovered that the Bible compared us to sheep. I grew up on a farm. I had met some sheep. I didn't want to be like a sheep. Sheep are the geekiest animals on earth. They run funny, they're frightened by the smallest disturbances, and they're so fragile they can actually die of fright.

I wanted to be compared to a lion but that role was taken. The Bible compares the devil to a lion. Maybe a hawk? Nope! Nowhere in the Bible are humans compared to hawks. I would've settled for a German shepherd, but a thorough search proved that "German shepherd" doesn't appear in the Bible anywhere either.

Turns out we are exactly like sheep. We easily wander away, we tend to move in flocks, we are easily frightened and fragile. Our life can be shortened by disease, trauma and, yes, even fear. Our only hope is in *the* good Shepherd.

He is a sheep's only source of safety, strength, and salvation.

How cool. Even though "all we like sheep have gone astray" and in spite of the fact that we are weak and vulnerable, in the arms of the Shepherd a "geeky sheep" becomes a "Super Sheep," capable of living in the power of Christ's resurrection.

We all, like sheep, have gone astray,
each of us has turned to our own way (Isaiah 53:6).

I can do all things through Christ who strengthens me
(Philippians 4:13, NKJV).

IT'S A DOG'S WORLD

There is a reason a dog is a man's best friend. That's because there are few animals on the face of the earth that are more loving and forgiving. As much as cats are loved, they have never been referred to as a man's best friend.

It's all about attitude. Pet a dog and look into his eyes. It's a look of worship. You can almost hear the dog whisper, "You are God."

Pet a cat and you will hear it's motor start. You may be tempted to believe he has the same worshipful spirit as the dog—until you look into your cat's eyes. You will almost hear him whisper, "I am God." Even you cat lovers know what I am saying is true. To a dog you're family. To a cat you're staff.

A dog doesn't care what you are wearing; he doesn't care what you smell like. In fact, the worse you smell, the more he loves you. He doesn't care if you come home late; he is just ecstatic that you are home.

The difference between a cat and a dog is the difference between pride and humility.

Proverbs 16:18 says, *"Pride goes before destruction, a haughty spirit before a fall."*

This is why cats had to learn to land on their feet. May your attitude today cause people to label you as "man's best friend."

SHINE!

Two small boys, not yet old enough to be in school, were overheard talking at the zoo one day.

"My name is Billy. What's yours?" asked the first boy.

"Tommy," replied the second.

"My daddy's an accountant. What does your daddy do for a living?" asked Billy.

Tommy replied, "My daddy's a lawyer."

"Honest?" asked Billy.

"No, just the regular kind," replied Tommy.

All of us have heard jokes or stories that involve a stereotype: the shady lawyer, the dumb blonde, the unbearable mother-in-law. I have often wondered where those stereotypes got started. How does a group of people take on a reputation that everyone in the group may not deserve? Is it possible the behavior of a few has tainted the reputation of the entire group?

As a follower of Christ, I am distressed to see Christians portrayed as unforgiving, mean-spirited, gullible people. Where did that come from? Have we encouraged the stereotype by our behavior?

Matthew 5:16 says, *"Let your light shine before others, that they may see your good works and glorify your Father in heaven."*

Lord, I pray that I will not contribute to any misguided perception of what it means to follow Christ. When people see me, please let them get a glimpse of you.

GO DEEPER: EPHESIANS 5:1-20

WILD RIDE

A teenager who had just received her learner's permit offered to drive her parents to church. After a hair-raising ride, they finally reached their destination. When the mother got out of the car, she said emphatically, "Thank you!"

"Anytime," her daughter replied with a smile.

As the mother headed for the church door, she said to her daughter, "I wasn't talking to you. I was talking to God."

I can identify with this woman. I taught my girls to drive in the empty parking lot of a mall. It wasn't big enough; the salt flats of Utah wouldn't have been big enough!

I thought I was a good teacher. I didn't complain about the whiplash I got as they tried to let out the clutch. I didn't scream when we jumped a curb and wiped out the small decorative tree that had done nothing to deserve such an end. But I did call out to God several times. I also thanked God that the parking lot was empty.

I wonder how God feels as He watches us careen through life as we learn to live for Him. I wonder if sometimes He slaps His forehead and whispers, *Thank... myself*, and then waits patiently for us to thank Him too.

Give thanks to the LORD, for he is good; his love endures forever (Psalm 107:1).

Since we are receiving a kingdom that cannot be shaken, let us be thankful, and so worship God acceptably with reverence and awe (Hebrews 12:28).

Even when the ride is wild, you never give up on us, Lord. For that, we thank you.

THE "D" WORD

A little boy would not settle down during a church service. He kept kicking the pew and defiantly throwing hymnals to the floor. The last straw came when he pulled the hair of the woman sitting in front of him. His father grabbed him by the arm and began marching him down the aisle toward the back of the church. The preacher didn't miss a beat until the dad reached the back of the church.

That's when the boy turned and yelled, "Y'all pray for me!"

That pretty much ended the service.

We live in a culture that despises the D word: *discipline*. They equate it with punishment. But there is a difference.

- Discipline motivates; punishment mortifies.
- Discipline is based on trust; punishment is based on fear.
- Discipline is time-in; punishment is time-out.
- Discipline is practice; punishment is penalty.

I despise cruel punishment and abuse as much as

anyone, but without discipline a society dies. Listen to what Proverbs has to say about discipline:

- A fool despises wisdom and discipline.
- Do not despise the Lord's discipline; do not resent His rebuke.
- He who hates correction will die.
- Whoever loves discipline loves knowledge, but he who hates correction is stupid. (This may be my favorite.)

The Bible says, *"No discipline is enjoyable while it is happening—it's painful! But afterward there will be a peaceful harvest of right living for those who are trained in this way"* (Hebrews 12:11 NLT).

Lord, I'm pretty sure I don't want to be stupid, and I'm certain that I want to live. Thank you for your loving discipline. Help me to learn and grow from it.

Go Deeper: Hebrews 12:5-13

WHAT'S ON THE INSIDE?

A little girl was misbehaving during an airline flight. She ran up and down the aisles without restraint. Finally, she climbed over an empty seat and fell. In the process, she kicked a man in the head.

The flight attendant told the flustered mom that her child had to be seated. The mom wrestled the child into her seat and pulled the seatbelt snuggly across the little girl's lap.

"You sit down and be still," the mom said, "or there will be a price to pay."

The little girl sat quietly with her arms folded and a smug smile on her face. Sensing some rebellion, the mom whispered, "Why are you smiling?"

"Because," the little girl said, "I may be sitting on the outside, but on the inside I am still running around."

Wow. I wonder how many people are sitting on the outside, but on the inside they are still running around.

Let this be my prayer today:

Search me, God, and know my heart;
test me and know my anxious thoughts.
See if there is any offensive way in me,
and lead me in the way everlasting
(Psalm 139:23-24).

ACTIONS SPEAK LOUDER THAN WORDS

During a game, a coach asked one of his young players, "Do you understand what cooperation is? What a team is?"

The little boy nodded yes.

"Do you understand that what matters is winning together as a team?"

The little boy nodded yes.

"So," the coach continued, "when a strike is called, or you are out at first, you don't argue or curse, or attack the umpire. Do you understand all that?"

Again, the boy nodded yes.

"Good," said the coach. "Now go over there and explain it to your mother."

In high school I witnessed the some of the most embarrassing behavior I've ever seen. At a basketball game, one of the players began to scream obscenities at the referee who had penalized him for a foul. Then the boy's father stormed onto the court and began a fist fight—first with the ref and then with a player from the opposing team. Even as a young boy, I remember making a connection between the actions of this parent and the poor sportsmanship that was often exhibited by his son.

Start children off on the way they should go, and even when they are old they will not turn from it (Proverbs 22:6).

Our children learn more from observing our behavior driving in rush-hour traffic than from many spoken words of wisdom. They trust us to model in our lives the principles we expect them to live by.

Lord, help me teach my children, with my words and actions.

READ BETWEEN THE LINES

When God created my youngest daughter, he gave her some of my twisted genes. I walked into the house one day to discover she had one end of a fishing line tied around her tooth and the other end tied to a door knob.

She was violently slamming the door trying to extract her tooth. With each swing of the door, I could hear the string make a "boing" sound as the line stretched to the breaking point. But the tooth held tight.

"What are you doing?" I demanded.

"I'm pulling my tooth."

I checked her tooth. "Your tooth isn't even loose!" I exclaimed.

"It will be," she announced and swung the door again. *Boing!*

"Quit it!" I demanded, "You're going to hurt yourself!"

"Leave me alone," she snapped, "I need money!" *Boing!*

That day I learned a valuable lesson. If you want to understand a child, you will need to learn to read between the lines. That's also good advice for understanding adults. Did you know that God reads between the lines every time we pray?

In the same way, the Spirit helps us in our weakness. We do not know what we ought to pray for, but the Spirit himself intercedes for us through wordless groans. And he who searches our hearts knows the mind of the Spirit, because the Spirit intercedes for God's people in accordance with the will of God (Romans 8:26-27).

Thank you, Jesus, for reading between the lines of my prayers and bringing the edited version our Father.

THE PROTECTIVE FATHER

I remember when boys began coming to our home to see my oldest daughter. I would occasionally answer the door carrying a butcher knife or sledge hammer. I would ask random questions like, "What is your tolerance for pain?" or, "Have you heard if anyone found the last boy who came here?" All this was done as a futile effort to protect my daughter.

To my daughter's embarrassment, this unusual welcome was followed by an interrogation. "Where are you going? What time will you be back? What are your intentions?" I probably shouldn't have worried so much; she was only seven years old at the time. You should have seen how bad it got when she became a teenager!

We parents work overtime to protect our children. God our Father is no different. He is trying to protect us from a far greater enemy. He knows the destructive intentions of the deceiver and warns us to be vigilant.

Be alert and of sober mind. Your enemy the devil prowls around like a roaring lion looking for someone to devour (1 Peter 5:8).

What Satan offers looks so appealing until we are reminded of his ultimate goal. Heed your heavenly Father's warning. Remember the price He paid to set you free. Welcome His loving protection and live!

YOU CAN'T HIDE THE TRUTH

If you ask people what they believe, they will often drone on for hours. But if you really want to discover what they believe, you only need watch what they do!

What people believe has little to do with what they say they believe and everything to do with how they behave.

Picture yourself walking down a path at night. A large Rottweiler approaches you on the path. It's too dark to tell what it is, but you believe it's a bear. Your brain will instantly send a text to your feet: "Run! It's a bear!" In that moment it doesn't matter whether it's a bear, a piece of cardboard, or a shadow. If you believe it's a bear, your feet will not argue with your brain. Your body will turn inside out in an effort to bolt in the opposite direction.

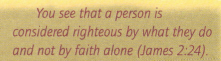

You see that a person is considered righteous by what they do and not by faith alone (James 2:24).

A person's behavior will follow what is really in his or her heart! If our actions don't match our words, it may be time for checkup.

Go Deeper: James 2

100

REST

I just spent a sleepless night in a hotel room with an air conditioner that sounded like a pterodactyl suffering from an abscessed tooth.

I kept thinking how the air conditioner must be related to the ironing board in the same room. If the sound of opening a hotel ironing board doesn't raise the hair on the back of your neck, you don't have a neck. And why is it that even the nicest hotels have heating and cooling systems that sound like a major car wreck when they stop and start—*All. Night. Long!*

Am I alone here?

Have you ever had one of those nights when you lie awake thinking, *If I go to sleep now, I will still have five hours of rest.* That kind of countdown continues until you fall asleep about thirty minutes before the alarm rings.

On mornings like that, I am lucky to make it to the airport. I feel like a snail wearing handcuffs. I forget things like taking a shower, brushing my teeth, or getting dressed.

Matthew 11:28 says, *"Come to me, all you who are weary and burdened, and I will give you rest."*

Oh sweet rest! Thank God that His rest is available even when we can't sleep. I've discovered that resting in Him helps me sleep better at night. Now I am praying He will do something about the air conditioner.

SOMEONE ELSE'S PAIN

A man said to the dentist, "I'm in a big hurry. I have two buddies waiting for us to go deer hunting, so forget about the anesthetic. I don't have time for the gums to get numb. Just pull the tooth and be done with it! We have our deer feeders set to go off in thirty minutes. I don't have time to wait for the anesthetic to work!"

The dentist thought to himself, *Surely, this is a very brave man asking to have his tooth pulled without using anything to kill the pain.*

So the dentist asked him, "Which tooth is it, sir?"

The man turned to his wife and said, "Open your mouth, honey, and show him."

My wife didn't think this joke was funny. But it does point out we are often insensitive to the pain someone else is experiencing but extremely sensitive when we are the one experiencing it. It is easy to watch other people and make a judgment about how they handle difficulty. Yet if we were in the same circumstance, we would likely weigh our judgment more carefully.

It becomes a different story when we put skin on it. Especially our own skin! So, when you see other people going through difficulty, open wide and think about how you would feel in that situation.

The author of Hebrews instructed Christians who were living under persecution to show love to each other.

Continue to remember those in prison as if you were together with them in prison, and those who are mistreated as if you yourselves were suffering (Hebrews 13:3).

You won't need anesthetic to follow that advice, but you might need a good shot of God's grace.

Please open my eyes today, Lord. Help me see the pain of others and respond in love.

CHILDREN

A lady walked into the doctor's office and said, "Doctor, I'd like you to evaluate my thirteen-year-old son."

Immediately the doctor said, "Okay, he's suffering from a transient psychosis with an intermittent rage disorder, punctuated by episodic radical mood swings, but his prognosis is good for full recovery."

The astounded mother said, "How can you say all that without even meeting him?"

The doctor said, "I thought you said he's thirteen?"

This note was recently discovered in a doctor's medical notations: "Patient has two teenage children, but no other abnormalities."

Someone said that when children reach the age of five, we should put them in a barrel and feed them through a small hole in the barrel. When they enter junior high, we should weld the barrel shut.

One day when I asked my young daughter why she was so difficult at home, she responded, "Because I can be." She explained that our home was the only place she dared vent her feelings and know she would still be loved. That brought tears to my eyes. So, I put down the welding torch and let her out of the barrel. Now she is a grown woman with two children of her own.

She wants to borrow the barrel.

Of course all of this is an exaggeration of a real truth! Parenting is a difficult and serious business, and children can take us to the limits of our emotions and sometimes our endurance. They also take us to an understanding of faith.

Truly I tell you, anyone who will not receive the kingdom of God like a little child will never enter it (Luke 18:17).

Lord give me the wisdom of a sage, the patience of a saint, and the faith of a child.

PAID IN FULL

A doctor and a lawyer were talking at a party. Their conversation was constantly interrupted by people describing their ailments and asking the doctor for medical advice. After an hour of this, the exasperated doctor asked the lawyer, "What do you do to stop people from asking you for legal advice when you're out of the office?"

"I give it to them," replied the lawyer, "and then I send them a bill."

The doctor was shocked, but agreed to give it a try. The next day, feeling slightly guilty, he prepared bills for all the people at the party who had asked him a question about their health. When he went to place them in his mailbox, he found a bill from the lawyer.

Now hear this, folks: If you have trusted Jesus, you will never get a bill from God. Not that there isn't a debt to be paid. The Bible says that the payment for sin is death, but Christ paid that debt when He went to the cross.

You can ask Him for advice, bring your problems to Him, confess all you have done. No invoice, no bill, no collection agency; instead, He offers grace and eternal life. Go ahead; check the letter He left for us.

If we confess our sins, he is faithful and just and will forgive us our sins and purify us from all unrighteousness (1 John 1:9).

Thank you for tearing up my invoice on the cross. Help me to live debt free.

CHILDREN OF GOD

In Sunday school one morning, little Joey raised his hand and asked a question that had perplexed him for some time.

"Mr. Jenkins," the little boy said, "there's something I can't figure out. According to the Bible, the children of Israel crossed the Red Sea, right?"

"Right."

"And the children of Israel beat up the Philistines, right?"

"Er, right."

"And the children of Israel built the temple, right?"

"Again, you're right."

"And the children of Israel fought the Egyptians, and the children of Israel were always doing something important for God, right?"

"All that is right, too," agreed Mr. Goldblatt. "So what's your question, Joey?"

"What were all the grownups doing?"

I love the fact that God referred to His people as children of Israel, and I love the fact that when we have trusted Christ, we are referred to as His sons and daughters.

So in Christ Jesus you are all children of God through faith (Galatians 3:26).

We are God's children.

No title on earth carries such tenderness, such responsibility, and such power. To answer Joey's question, hopefully we grownups are living up to our royal title, fighting for what is right, and helping other grownups become God's children too.

HIDDEN TREASURE

On the first day of school, the teacher advised the class that each school day would start with the Pledge of Allegiance. She instructed the children to put their right hand over their heart and repeat after her.

As she started to recite— "I pledge allegiance to the flag …"—the teacher looked around the room and noticed that Andy had his right hand over the right side of his bottom.

She stopped and said, "Andy, I cannot continue until you put your hand over your heart."

Andy looked up and said, "It is over my heart."

After several more attempts to get Andy to put his hand over his heart, the teacher asked, "Why do you think that is your heart, Andy?"

Andy answered, "Because every time my grandma comes to visit, she pats me there and says, 'Bless your little heart,' and Grandma never lies."

Think about this for a moment. The place Andy had his hand is the same place we carry our wallet.

When I heard this story, I couldn't help but think of Matthew 6:21: "For where your treasure is, there your heart will be also."

Perhaps as we recite "one nation, under God," it would be proper to raise our hands toward heaven. Hopefully that's where our treasure and our heart reside.

GO DEEPER: MATTHEW 6:19-34

LEAVE IT THERE!

oday there is an entire industry built around stress management. One young lady confidently walked around the room while leading a stress management seminar. She raised a glass of water, and everyone knew she was going to ask the ultimate question, "Is this glass half empty or half full?'"

But she fooled them all. "How heavy is this glass of water?" she asked with a smile.

Answers called out ranging from 8 oz. to 20 oz. Then she said, "The absolute weight doesn't matter. It depends on how long I hold it. If I hold it for a minute, that's not a problem. If I hold it for an hour, I'll have an ache in my right arm. If I hold it for a day, you'll have to call an ambulance. In each case it's the same weight, but the longer I hold it, the heavier it becomes."

She continued, "That's the way it is with stress. If we carry our burdens all the time, sooner or later, as the burdens become increasingly heavy, we won't be able to carry on."

Worry and stress do not solve the problem; they dissolve our strength.

I am reminded of an old hymn that has a great solution to stress management. The lyrics say, "Take your burden to the Lord and leave it there."[7] The refrain to that song repeats "leave it there" four times!

Evidently the writer wanted to burn these words on our hearts. Too often we take our burdens to the Lord and then drag them back home again.

Give your burdens to the LORD,
and he will take care of you (Psalm 55:22, NLT).

Before you start this day, take your burdens to the Lord and leave them there!

[7]Charles A. Tindley, "Leave It There," 1916.

GUARD YOUR TONGUE

A little old lady answered a knock on the door and was confronted by a well-dressed young man carrying a vacuum cleaner.

"Good morning," said the young man. "If I could take a couple minutes of your time, I would like to demonstrate the very latest in high-powered vacuum cleaners."

"Go away!" said the old lady. "I'm broke and haven't got any money!" and she proceeded to close the door.

Quick as a flash, the young man wedged his foot in the door and pushed it wide open. "Don't be too hasty!" he said. "Not until you have at least seen my demonstration."

And with that, he emptied the contents of a cat litter box onto her hallway carpet.

"Now," he boasted, "if this vacuum cleaner doesn't remove all traces of this cat litter from your carpet in the next five minutes, madam, I will personally eat the remainder."

The old lady stepped back and said, "Well, let me get you a fork, 'cause they cut off my electricity this morning."[8]

Do you ever speak before you think? Have you ever spoken words quickly that you wished you could take back? Too often we put both feet in our mouth and end up without a leg to stand on.

Those who guard their mouths and their tongues keeps themselves from calamity (Proverbs 21:23).

[8]Used with permission Mikey's Funnies, www.MikeysFunnies.com.

THE STATE OF CONFUSION

Does life occasionally come at you so fast that you lose your equilibrium? I've lived so long I often wonder if my brain cells have moved to another state: the state of confusion.

I was in that state when I left a meeting at church. As I walked through the building I did that little Macarena dance we all do, patting each pocket to be sure we have everything we came with. In the middle of the dance, I froze. My keys were not in my pocket.

Evidently, I had left them in the car. I walked out the door and froze again. My car was gone. Someone had stolen my car.

I quickly made a call to the police and reported the car stolen, and then made the scariest call of all. I called Diane to tell her what I had done.

When she answered the phone, I confessed. "Honey, I'm sorry. I left the keys in the car, and it has been stolen."

"Ken," she said incredulously, "I dropped you off!"

That explained where my car had gone! Now, hopefully, she can tell me where my brain is.

If you are living in the "state of confusion," be encouraged; you're not alone. I have even met young people who live there. You may not remember who drops you off, just don't forget that God never will forget.

> *The LORD your God goes with you; he will never leave you nor forsake you (Deuteronomy 31:6).*

THE CURE TO INSOMNIA

The bags under my eyes are too big to fit in the overhead compartment on an airliner.

It's because I sleep like a baby: accosted by nightmares, distressed by nature's call, and up crying half the night.

I tried a Memory Foam mattress. I didn't sleep any better, but in the morning the bed's memory retained an indentation the perfect shape of my body. At least I now have my own personal fossil.

I tried a Sleep Number bed and lay awake all night doing the math. My sleep number is 90. That's the number of seconds I actually sleep each night.

My flesh is willing, but my mind is weak. My body begs, "Oh these sheets feel so good; let's go to sleep." But my mind argues, "Nope, tonight we're going to review all your sins and plan the rest of your life."

Finally, I manage to fall asleep about the same time my bladder wakes up. It's a lose-lose proposition. Here are some suggestions for sleeping well.

- Buy a pacifier. It seems to work for my grandchildren.

- Have someone read you a story: preferably someone who wants to stay awake.

- Listen to the recording of an old sermon. I've seen that put people to sleep.

Here's a better one.

Pray!

If I start to pray, it isn't long until I go out like a light. At first I didn't know if it was the peace of the Lord or the devil who knocked me out. I do know that there is a calm that takes over when we talk to God. In His presence the stress of the day drifts away. Actually, prayer is much more than just a sleep aid.

Pray without ceasing, give thanks in all circumstances; for this is the will of God in Christ Jesus for you (1 Thessalonians 5:17-18, ESV).

Try it! Is there a better place to go to sleep than in the presence of God?

LOOKING FOR ACORNS

I was doing almost fifty miles an hour—downhill—on a bicycle. My wife, Diane, had warned me, "Don't go so fast! At that speed, if you hit an acorn, you're dead." I had never thought of that before. But now I had developed an acute fear of acorns. I was flying down the hill watching for any acorn that might put me over the handlebars. That's why I didn't see the dog.

He came out of a driveway snarling, headed straight for my ankles. I jerked the handle bars and started a violent shimmy in the front wheel of the bike. Fortunately, when I applied the brakes, the shimmy stopped. Unfortunately, the dog started to catch up to me.

I looked back at his bared fangs. That's when I hit the acorn.

I lay on the pavement groaning in pain and waiting for the dog to grab my throat. But the dog was yelping and running home with his tail between his legs.

I don't know if it was the sound of the crash that scared him or the up-close sight of me in spandex bike shorts, but I never saw him again. Thankfully, my injuries were minor, and I had a bike I could ride home.

That night I recalled a Bible verse: *"Stay alert! Watch out for your great enemy, the devil. He prowls around like a roaring lion, looking for someone to devour" (1 Peter 5:8, NLT).*

Good advice to start this day. Be alert for the devil and vicious dogs.

Wouldn't hurt to slow down and watch for acorns too.

GOOD NEWS

Remember the old saying "no news is good news"? It may be true. It's a reporter's job to hunt for bad news.

Someone said that the evening news always begins with "Good evening," and then proceeds to tell you why it isn't. The evening news can be the most depressing thirty minutes of television programming in the day. Dire warnings about killer diseases like swine flu, bird flu, and Asian flu, and of course there's that "one flu over the cuckoo's nest."

The world scurries in panic, even though the normal variety of flu kills more people than all of panic flus put together. But that's old news and not nearly as scary and depressing.

There are reports about drive-by shootings, war, and world financial collapse. Watching the news makes us believe there must not be any good news.

But the greatest news of all isn't heard on network news channels; it's found in the pages of your Bible.

For God so loved the world that he gave his one and only Son, that whoever believes in him shall not perish but have eternal life (John 3:16).

Jesus came to save sinners. His grace and love continues to create good news all over the world. Since the networks won't proclaim it you do it.

"Good evening. 'This is the day the LORD has made; we will rejoice and be glad in it.' Good night." (See Psalm 118:24, NKJV).

GOD ANSWERS PRAYER

As I settled into my airplane seat I noticed the lady sitting next to me was wearing an exquisite pair of earrings. "Where did you get those earrings?" I asked, "They are beautiful. I would love to buy a pair for my wife."

The lady said thank you, put on some earphones, and began listening to music. *Whoa!* Had I been too bold? Was my question inappropriate? Did I appear to be a bumbling old man looking for a date? I felt awkward and unwilling to risk further embarrassment. I buried my head in a book.

About an hour later, the captain announced that we were preparing to land. The young lady took off her earphones, tapped me on the shoulder, and said, "Men's Warehouse!" I didn't know what she was talking about and it must have showed. She smiled. "I got the earrings at Men's Warehouse." *Wow*. By the time she answered the question, I had forgotten I asked it.

As I deplaned, I thought of how often I pray only to despair because there is no immediate answer. Then days, weeks, or years later God answers the prayer. Not always in the way or the time frame I expected. But my prayer is answered.

This little saying is on a plaque that hangs in our kitchen: "God has three answers to every prayer: Yes, not yet, and I have something better in mind."

This is the confidence we have in approaching God: that if we ask anything according to his will, he hears us (1 John 5:14).

GO DEEPER: LUKE 11:5-10

FOR THE SICK

A little girl was in church with her mother when she started feeling ill. "Mommy," she said, "can we leave now?"

"No," her mother whispered, "We have to wait till church is over."

After a few minutes, the little girl said, "Mom, I think I have to throw up!"

"Then go out the front door and around to the back of the church, and throw up behind a bush," the mom instructed.

After about sixty seconds, the little girl returned to her seat. "Did you throw up?" the mom asked.

The little girl whispered yes.

"How could you have gone all the way outside and returned so quickly?"

The little girl answered, "I didn't have to go out of the church, Mommy. They have a box next to the front door that says, "'For the Sick.'"

Many people jump from church to church looking for one attended by people who have no problems. My pastor said we shouldn't look for a church with perfect people because if we ever join one, we'll ruin it.

"It is not the healthy who need a doctor, but the sick. I have not come to call the righteous, but sinners" *(Mark 2:17).*

That's a group I can identify with.

He came so that we might be healed, but it might take awhile, so let's keep that sign at the back of the church—"For the Sick."

THE TRUTH

The old proverb "The truth will find you out" is true. The truth does not retreat where lies proliferate; rather, it patiently waits for time to erode the loose edges of a lie and eventually truth is revealed.

When my daughter was young, she tried to convince me our cat had come into her room and wet her bed. She couldn't see how silly her little white lie sounded. When I told her the cat had been outside all night, she informed me that it had pulled off the screen from the outside, sneaked into the room, wet her bed, and then jumped back out the window.

She saw me staring at the window and quickly added that on his way out the cat had put the screen back. When she finally confessed, she discovered there was no penalty for wetting the bed, but there were consequences for lying. Our family puts a premium on telling the truth.

A boss called one of his employees into the office and asked. "Do you believe in life after death?"

"Yes sir," the clerk replied.

"That's good," the boss said. "After you left early yesterday to go to your grandmother's funeral, she stopped in to see you."

Guide me in your truth and teach me,
for you are God my Savior,
and my hope is in you all day long
(Psalm 25:5).

Lord help me tell the truth today, the whole truth, and nothing but the truth.

GO DEEPER: EPHESIANS 4:17-32

OBLIVIOUS

My flight leveled off at 30,000 feet, so I took out my laptop to begin working when suddenly the seat in front of me flew back propelling the head of the young women in front of me to within inches of my face.

These are not reclining seats; they're deadly weapons. My laptop slammed shut on my fingers. The woman was oblivious to anyone around her. She didn't hear the laptop slam or my scream of pain. This was going to be a long flight.

What could be worse? Hair. That's what! She began running her hands through her long, blond hair and throwing the tangled mass over the back of her seat toward me. I wondered when it would stop. I wondered if small creatures that lived in that tawny forest were now finding a new home on me. I longed for the days when they still allowed scissors on the flight.

I was about to protest when I was reminded of how many times I have been inconsiderate of those around me: unthinkingly cutting in line, or speaking loudly on my cell phone in a public place. I never intended disrespect or harm. I was blind to the needs of others. In that moment it was all about me.

Be devoted to one another in love. Honor one another above yourselves (Romans 12:10).

That is a worthy goal Paul set for believers. It is also an honorable way to treat every one.

GO DEEPER: 1 CORINTHIANS 13:1-7

MOVING FORWARD

Remember life before the computer, when memory was something you lost with old age? Remember when an application was for employment, and you could actually find it?

Before the computer, a program was a television show and a cursor was a person who used profanity. Remember when a keyboard was a piano, the web was behind your refrigerator, a virus was the flu, and a CD was a bank account?

I remember when a hard drive was a long, difficult trip on the road, and a mouse pad was where a mouse lived.

Maybe I am getting old, but there are times I long for books with actual pages and handwritten letters. I wish spam still came in a can, packed with that nasty wiggly gelatin.

Those days are gone, and we have a choice. We can stare wistfully into the past, longing for what was and never again will be, or we can use every advancement in technology to bring the good news of God's love to the world today. Let's choose the last option.

Those who stare into the past back blindly into the future. Author unknown

WORDS MAKE A DIFFERENCE

"How many times have I told you...?" Those words were usually uttered by my parents after I had suffered the consequences of some less-than-brilliant behavior, like when my dog bit me. "How many times have I told you not to lick the dog's face?"

"I don't care if he licked your face first. If I've told you once, I've told you a thousand times, don't lick the dog's face."

I learned early in life never to answer the question "How many times have I told you..." I didn't know it was a rhetorical question until I answered, "Well, it has to be somewhere between once and a thousand; I'll guess 901." That was the wrong answer. I never did learn the right number, but after that day I decided I wouldn't venture any more guesses.

Many people grow up with sad memories of words they

heard at home: "Get out of my sight." "I wish you had never been born." Others remember humorous words like, "If you keep doing that, your face will stay that way."

What words are you leaving for your children to remember? "I love you"? "I am proud of you"? "God loves you"? Those will be a source of strength to your children all of their lives.

Fathers, do not exasperate your children; instead, bring them up in the training and instruction of the Lord (Ephesians 6:4).

Go Deeper: Deuteronomy 6:4-7

GOD'S MEMORY LOSS

Two middle-aged couples were enjoying friendly conversation when one of the men asked the other, "Fred, how was the memory clinic you went to last month?"

Fred got all excited and said, "It was outstanding! They taught us all the latest psychological techniques for memory, like visualization, association, and so on. It was great. I haven't had a problem since."

Fred's friend said, "Sounds like something I could use. What was the name of the clinic?"

Fred went blank. He thought and thought, but couldn't remember.

Then a smile broke across his face and he asked, "What do you call that flower with the long stem and thorns?"

His friend said, "You mean a rose?"

"Yes, that's it!" He turned to his wife, "Hey, Rose, what was the name of that memory clinic?"

Did you know that God has a memory problem? The Lord says,

I will forgive their wickedness and will remember their sins no more (Jeremiah 31:34).

Wow! God chooses to forget the sins of those who have trusted His Son. Embrace His offer of forgiveness, obey His direction for your life, and lighten up and live.

STAY OFF THE GRASS

I remember the day I managed to walk through a field of tall grass infested with chiggers. For those of you who don't know what a chigger is, it is a tiny bug you can't see that loves to do exploratory drilling on your body.

The itching from chigger bites drives one mad. I would rather have a root canal than a chigger bite, and I had about fifty of them.

Friends said to put fingernail polish on the bites. It doesn't work. The chiggers' nails looked great, but my legs still itched like crazy. A friend gave me great advice: if you live in Tennessee, stay out of the tall grass.

This advice was wise and simple and applies to many aspects of life. It is also some of the most ignored advice on earth. When I was young, many wise and caring mentors warned me about behavior and situations that should be avoided. I foolishly thought I was immune to whatever dangers lurked there. I got bit, and I paid a high price for ignoring the good advice.

Perhaps you are a better learner. So here is my advice. If you live on earth, avoid situations where you may be ensnared by the deceiver. Stay out of the grass.

Submit yourselves, then, to God. Resist the devil, and he will flee from you (James 4:7).

Lord, I am yours today. Give me the wisdom to see every move the deceiver makes, the power to rebuke him in your name and rejoice as I watch him run away.

LIFE MAKES US HUMBLE

There are some things that make me feel stupid, like when I wave across the room to someone I think I recognize only to discover that they have no idea who I am. I feel even dumber when I continue to wave, pretending to look past them at someone else. That often attracts the attention of another stranger who thinks I must be a stalker or a poor soul desperately in need of friendship.

A few years ago, I got on an airplane and found that someone was sitting in my seat. The person showed me his ticket. We had been assigned the same seat. Indignant at the airline's careless mistake, I strode up to the flight attendant, showed her the error, and insisted that it be corrected.

Loud enough so that most of the passengers could hear, she announced that I was on the wrong airplane. Sometimes I think I should just wear a sign that says, "Idiot in search of a village."

I once came out of a supermarket and climbed into the wrong car with a woman I had never met. You should have seen the look on that woman's face. You should have seen the look on my wife's face. No use trying to explain that the cars looked alike.

Diane says this is God's way of keeping me humble. I still think I need the "Idiot" sign. All of this simply confirms that we are not as cool as we think we are. It also gives us motivation not judge the actions of others so harshly.

When pride comes, then comes disgrace,
but with humility comes wisdom (Proverbs 11:2).

Lord, help me know the difference between the pride that is opposite of shame and to not be ashamed. Help me know the pride that is opposite of humility and give me the wisdom to give you the glory for every good thing in my life.

131

HONESTY

What does it cost to tell the truth? A little boy tells it this way:

Our teacher asked us what our favorite animal was, and I said, "Fried chicken." She said I wasn't funny. But she couldn't have been right—everyone else in the class laughed.

My parents told me to always be truthful, and I am. Fried chicken is my favorite animal. I told my dad, and he said my teacher was probably a member of PETA. He said they love animals very much. I do too—especially chicken, pork, and beef.

Anyway, my teacher sent me to the principal's office. I told him what happened, and he laughed too. Then he told me not to do it again.

The next day my teacher asked me what my favorite live animal was. I told her it was chicken. She asked me why. I told her it was because you could make them into fried chicken. She sent me back to the principal's office. He laughed and told me not to do it again.

I don't understand. My parents taught me to be honest, but my teacher doesn't like it when I am. Today, my teacher asked us to tell her what famous person we admire most.

I told her, "Colonel Sanders."

Guess where I am now...

Paul did prison time for telling the truth. Christ went to the cross for telling the truth. Evidently truth is a valuable commodity. Perhaps that's because of the source.

Jesus said, *"If you hold to my teaching, you are really my disciples. Then you will know the truth, and the truth will set you free" (John 8:31-32).*

GENEROSITY

A pastor told his congregation that the church needed some extra money. He asked the people to consider donating a little more than usual. He said that whoever gave the most would be able to pick out three hymns. After the offering plates were passed, the pastor glanced down and noticed that someone had placed a $1,000 bill in the offering.

He was so excited that he immediately shared his joy with his congregation and said he'd like to personally thank the person who placed the money in the plate. A very quiet, elderly, saintly looking lady all the way in the back shyly raised her hand. The pastor asked her to come to the front.

Slowly she made her way to the front. He told her how wonderful it was that she gave so much. To thank her, he asked her to pick out three hymns.

Her eyes brightened as she looked over the congregation, pointed to the three most handsome men in the building and said, "I'll take him and him and him."

It is rare to find a person who gives expecting nothing in return. The Pharisees made a public spectacle of their giving so they would be noticed. I have met only a few people who give for the sheer joy of giving. They do get something in return: the desire to give even more.

Each of you should give what you have decided in your heart to give, not reluctantly or under compulsion, for God loves a cheerful giver (2 Corinthians 9:7).

Lighten up your wallet and live.

GO DEEPER: 2 CORINTHIANS 9:6-15

MARINE MAGIC

As the crowded airliner was about to take off, the peace was shattered by a five-year-old boy who threw a wild temper tantrum. No matter what his frustrated, embarrassed mother did to try to calm him down, the boy continued to scream furiously and kick the seats around him.

Suddenly, from the rear of the plane, an elderly man in a Marine uniform slowly walked up the aisle. Calming the flustered mother with an upraised hand, the white-haired, soft-spoken Marine leaned down and, motioning toward the medals on his chest, whispered something into the boy's ear.

Instantly, the boy calmed down, gently took his mother's hand, and quietly fastened his seat belt. All the other passengers burst into spontaneous applause.

As the Marine slowly made his way back to his seat, one of the cabin attendants asked, "Excuse me, sir, what magic words did you say to calm that little boy?"

The Marine smiled serenely and gently confided, "I showed him my pilot's wings, service stars, and battle ribbons, and explained that they entitle me to throw one passenger out the plane door on any flight I choose."

Earth is populated with rebellious, unruly humans, and God is entitled to throw out the whole lot. Yet, thank God, His message is different than that of the elderly Marine.

God presented Christ as a sacrifice of atonement, through the shedding of his blood—to be received by faith (Romans 3:25).

Buckle up and enjoy the ride.

Go Deeper: Romans 3:9-26

LIVE LOUD

Harry realized he needed to purchase a hearing aid, but he was unwilling to spend much money. "How much do they cost?" he asked the salesperson.

"That depends," he said. "They run from $2 to $2,000."

Harry was pretty tight with his money so he said, "Let's see the $2 model."

The salesperson put the device around his neck. "You just stick this big red button in your ear and run this wire down to your pocket," he instructed.

"How does it work?" asked Harry.

"For $2 it doesn't work," the salesperson replied. "But when people see it on you, they'll talk louder."

I realize this is a stretch, but when I first heard this joke I thought of how the same economic principle applies to our witness. We can spend thousands of dollars and hundreds of hours getting a seminary degree. We can purchase a huge Bible and carry it everywhere we go. We might wear colorful T-shirts and sport bumper stickers with a witty Christian message.

But ultimately it is our love for others that will enable people to hear our message much more clearly.

Jesus told His disciples, *"By this everyone will know that you are my disciples, if you love one another"* (John 13:35).

He didn't even have t-shirts for sale!

DON'T DO THAT

Jim had been seeing a psychoanalyst for treatment of his lifelong fear of monsters under his bed. It had been years since he had gotten a good night's sleep. He wasn't making any progress, so he terminated his therapy sessions and decided to try something different.

A few weeks later, Jim's former psychoanalyst ran into him on the street and was surprised to find him looking so well-rested, relaxed, and cheerful. "Doc!" Jim said, "It's amazing! I'm cured!"

"That's great news!" the psychoanalyst said. "You certainly do seem to be doing much better. What happened?"

"I went to see a behaviorist," Jim said, "and he cured me in just one session!"

"One session? How did a behaviorist cure you in one session?"

"Easy," said Jim. "He told me to saw the legs off my bed."

You may have heard about the man who went to the

doctor with pain in his arm. He turned his arm at a weird angle and told the doctor, "it hurts when I do this."

The doctor wrote something on his prescription pad, tore off the page and handed it to the patient. It read "Don't do that."

We often endure great suffering because we keep doing things that bring us pain. In John 8, there is an amazing story of a woman who faced great guilt and possible stoning because of her behavior. Jesus forgave her, and then said, "Now don't do that."

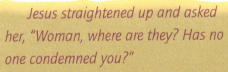

Jesus straightened up and asked her, "Woman, where are they? Has no one condemned you?"

"No one, sir," she said.

"Then neither do I condemn you," Jesus declared. "Go now and leave your life of sin" (John 8:10).

GO DEEPER: JOHN 8:2-11

OPPORTUNITY KNOCKS

I was about to be introduced as the keynote speaker at a major corporate convention when I realized that I had forgotten my notes in my room. I ran for the elevator and dived through the doors just as they closed. I pressed the button to the ninth floor and took a deep breath, trying to be lighter so the elevator would get there more quickly.

The elevator stopped at the ninth floor, but the doors didn't open. I pushed the button frantically. To my horror, the elevator started to move upward. It stopped at the fourteenth floor, but the doors still would not open. In full panic I began banging on the doors, shouting, "Someone call the front desk. The elevator doors are stuck."

Behind me a voice said, "No they aren't."

I whirled around to discover this was one of those elevators that had doors on both sides. There were seven people waiting to get on, but none of them wanted to get on with a crazy man kicking the door.

I made it back to the ballroom and gave my speech without notes. I told the audience that day, "If you find yourself kicking and screaming because a door won't open, look around. God may have another door of opportunity open just waiting for you to walk through."

Lord, keep me from tunnel vision. Help me keep my eyes open for whatever you want for my life today.

FROM THE MOUTHS OF BABES

Every parent should think twice before they invite a child to pray in public. A woman invited some people to dinner. At the table, she turned to her six-year-old daughter and said, "Would you like to say the blessing?"

"I wouldn't know what to say," the little girl replied

"Just say what you hear Mommy say," the mother said.

The little girl bowed her head and said, "Dear Lord, why on earth did I invite all these people to dinner?"

I bet that was an interesting dinner.

I think God loves the prayers of children. Once, my grandson was saying grace before a meal. He prayed for all the people who had died, all the animals that were out in the cold, all the animals that were too hot, missionaries, the president, his teacher, all the starving children... Finally with everyone at the table wondering how long this could possibly go on, his father nudged him and whispered,

"What about the food?"

Without hesitation my grandson said, "The food can wait." Then he continued praying for the rest of the universe.

One of my favorite prayers came from another little boy: "Dear God, please take care of my daddy and my mommy and my sister and my brother and my doggy and me. Oh, please take care of yourself, God. If anything happens to you, we're gonna be in a big mess."

From the mouths of babes!

Thank you God that you are alive and well, and that we can live with you forever.

SNEAKING OUT

When I was young, my friends at school always talked about sneaking out at night. It sounded like the coolest thing. So one night I stayed awake until my parents had gone to bed. I could hear my dad snoring and my mom's deep breathing. I knew they were sound asleep.

I slowly opened the window of my bedroom—my heart pounding. I was usually a compliant, well-behaved boy. This was the scariest, most defiant thing I had ever done. I crawled out the window onto the roof of our kitchen. I hung from the rain gutter and dropped to the ground. Then it hit me. We lived on a farm. There was no one around for miles. I had sneaked out into nothing. Waking my parents was the only way I could get back in.

So, I went out to the barn and milked the cows.

I wish I could say that was the only incident of rebellion in my life. My parents forgave me, but never let me forget the foolishness of my actions. I am happy to say that God went even further.

I, even I, am he who blots out your transgressions, for my own sake, and remembers your sins no more (Isaiah 43:25).

Thank you for your grace and mercy, dear Lord. Help me live today in grateful obedience.